ACTIVITIES UNLIMITED

CREATIVE AND EXCITING SENSORY MOTOR ACTIVITIES.

D1401248

A VERY SPECIAL THANKS TO

Our families who allowed us to spend many hours away from them in order to make this dream a reality. We dedicate this book to you for your patience, encouragement, and support.

THANKS!

Dick, Meghan, and Kevin
Junior and Cody
Meredith and Emily

ACTIVITIES UNLIMITED

by
Alexandra Cleveland
Barbara Caton
Lezlie Adler

Art
Janet McDonnell

A BUILDING BLOCKS Publication
38W567 Brindlewood, Elgin, Illinois 60123

© 1994

ISBN 0-943452-17-1

ART

Cover Design and Graphics   David VanDelinder
Studio 155
Elgin, Illinois 60120

Illustration   Janet McDonnell
Arlington Heights, Illinois 60004

Computer Graphics   Greg Wilmes
Elgin, Illinois 60123

Graphics Layout   David Jensen Design
Elgin, Illinois 60120

OUR SINCERE THANKS TO

...all the children who enthusiastically participated in these activities even when our ideas got a little goofy or messy.

...Kevin Caton for his computer expertise.

...Nicole Harlton for taking our photograph.

...Dorothy and Al Piangerelli for their countless hours of babysitting.

PUBLISHED BY:

BUILDING BLOCKS
38W567 Brindlewood
Elgin, Illinois 60123

ISBN 0-943452-17-1

DEDICATED TO

All the children who get involved in these activities!
May they have fantastic fun and lots of learning.

CONTENTS

FINE MOTOR ACTIVITIES

ORAL MOTOR ACTIVITIES

VISUAL CONTROL ACTIVITIES

GROSS MOTOR ACTIVITIES

INTRODUCTION

ACTIVITIES UNLIMITED was written to provide teachers, therapists (occupational, physical, speech), and parents with a ready resource filled with unique yet simple activities which promote, develop, and stimulate children's:

- CREATIVITY

- LANGUAGE

- UNDERSTANDING OF THEIR BODIES

- PERCEPTION

- GROSS MOTOR SKILLS

- FINE MOTOR SKILLS

- SELF-HELP SKILLS

- SOCIAL SKILLS

YOU'LL DISCOVER THAT THE ACTIVITIES ARE:

• Fun, innovative, and help you to teach age-appropriate skills in new ways, thus enabling you to make a real difference in children's development.

• Hands-on, open-ended, and developmentally appropriate, to insure success for all children no matter what their skill levels.

• Flexible so you can use them in your learning centers, with small and large groups, and/or while working with one child.

• Quickly engaging and easy for children to play on their own.

• Inherently motivating, thus keeping children involved for long periods of time.

• Easy and quick to set up, so you can use them anytime, anyplace in your school or home.

• Planned with inexpensive, and easy-to-get materials thus enabling you to offer a wide variety of activities with little concern for cost.

FINE MOTOR

Rubber Glove Fun

MATERIALS AND SUPPLIES

Surgical rubber gloves   Bird seed
Small pebbles   Sand
Packing peanuts   Water
Aquarium gravel   Cotton balls

Partially fill the rubber gloves with different ingredients. Tie them closed at the wrist. Put the gloves in your water table or the discovery table.

ACTIVITY

Let the children manipulate the gloves in their hands by squeezing them, rolling them around, holding and shaking them, and squeezing them between their palms. Encourage the children to exchange gloves and experience a variety of textures.

VARIATIONS:

Hot and Cold Gloves: Fill several gloves with very cold water and several with warm water. (Frozen gloves are especially fun.)

Pass the Gloves: Bring one or more gloves to group time. Pass the gloves to music. Stop the music. Have the children holding the gloves tell the others what might be in them. Start the music again and keep playing.

Plaster Sculptures

CHILDREN WILL DEVELOP
Hand Strength
Tactile Discrimination
Arm, Hand, Finger Coordination

USE WITH:
Individuals
Small Groups

MATERIALS AND SUPPLIES

Large bowl
Mixing spoon
Plaster of Paris
Resealable gallon-size plastic bags

Following the directions on the package, let the children help you mix the plaster of Paris with water. Set the plaster, spoon, and resealable bags on the table.

ACTIVITY

Let each child help you scoop some of the plaster mixture into a bag and seal it. Label each bag with each child's name written on it.

Have the children squeeze the bags noting the changes in temperature and consistency of the plaster mixture. The children can continue manipulating and forming the mixture for as long as they want or until the plaster hardens.

Open each bag and set them aside to let the plaster cure for a day or two. When the sculptures are completely dry, remove them from the bags and let the children paint them if they would like.

VARIATIONS:

Watercolor Sculptures: Add food coloring to the water.

Paint Sculptures: Glue the plaster sculptures onto styrofoam meat trays and paint the creations with water colors.

Collage Sculptures: Glue a variety of art materials such as feathers, sequins, pom-poms, etc. to the sculptures.

Wacky Water Table Fun

CHILDREN WILL DEVELOP
    Tactile Discrimination
    Arm, Hand, Finger Coordination
    Visual Motor Coordination

USE WITH:
    Individuals
    Small groups

MATERIALS AND SUPPLIES

Smocks	Food coloring	Funnels
Spoons	Perfume	Measuring containers
Scoops	Extracts	Tongs
Small containers	Small objects	Small shovels
Spray bottles	Extra-firm balloons, such	Gloves/mittens
Squirt bottles	as inflatable punch balls	Pie pans
Unbreakable eyedroppers	Popsicle sticks	

Choose the materials you need for the activity and put them in or near your water table. Remember smocks when the *"fun"* is messy.

CORNSTARCH OR FLOUR

Exploring Cornstarch/Flour: Allow the children time to explore the dry cornstarch or flour using their hands, spoons, and small containers.

Wet Cornstarch/Flour: Fill spray and squirt bottles with different temperatures of water. Let the children add water to the cornstarch/flour and then explore it with their hands. Add pie pans and spoons for additional exploration.

Colorful Cornstarch/Flour: Let the children add colored water to the flour/cornstarch using eye droppers.

AQUARIUM GRAVEL

Scoop and Pour: Have a variety of pouring and filling utensils, such as funnels, spoons, scoops, ladles, and measuring containers available to the children to use with the aquarium gravel.

Hide N' Seek: Hide objects, such as stringing beads or small colored blocks, in the aquarium gravel. Encourage the children to find them.

SHAVING CREAM

Exploring Shaving Cream: Encourage the children to explore the shaving cream by rubbing it on their arms, hands, and on the sides and bottom of the water table.

Colorful Shaving Cream: Add eye droppers and small containers of diluted food coloring to the activity. Let the children add drops of color the shaving cream.

Smelly Shaving Cream: Add scents to the shaving cream.

Hide 'N Seek: Hide objects in the shaving cream for the children to find.

Shaving: Inflate extra-firm balloons* of different sizes and shapes. Put them in the water table. Have the children carefully spread shaving cream on the balloons with their hands and then shave it off with popsicle sticks.
* *Remember Safety: Be sure to use extra-firm balloons, such as inflatable punch balls. Monitor the activity at all times. If a balloon should break remove it immediately.*

PACKING PEANUTS

Tong Pick Up: Using tongs, have the children fill containers with the packing peanuts and then dump them back into to the water table.

Hide N' Seek: Hide objects in the packing peanuts for the children to find.

More Tong Pick Up: Pour enough water in the water table so the packing peanuts float. Let the children pick them with tongs.

SNOW

Exploring Snow: Encourage the children to explore the snow using scoops, plastic containers, small shovels, etc. (Remember to have mittens available.)

Snow Sculptures: Have the children put on mittens or gloves to make snow balls, mountains, trails, snow people, and more.

Colorful Snow: Add eyedroppers and small containers of colored water to the activity. Let the children add drops of colored water to the snow

Dr. Spot

CHILDREN WILL DEVELOP
Finger Coordination
Eye-Hand Coordination
Visual Motor Coordination

USE WITH:
Individuals
Small groups

MATERIALS AND SUPPLIES

Several trays of watercolor paints
Small water containers
Paper

Put trays of water colors, water containers, and paper on the art table.

ACTIVITY

Have the children wet their fingertips, press them in the different colors of paint, and make colored spots by pressing their fingertips all over the paper. Let the children continue to make fingerprints for as long as they would like.

VARIATIONS:

Brighter Dr. Spot: Use fingerpaints instead of water colors.

Connect The Spots: Put fine-tipped markers and/or crayons on the table. As the children are making spots, encourage them to keep the spots separate. After the children have made all of the spots they want and they have dried, let the children connect the spots with markers. Maybe the children would like to make even more spots and connect them.

Button Rub

CHILDREN WILL DEVELOP
    Tactile Discrimination
    Arm, Hand, Finger Coordination

USE WITH:
    Individuals
    Small groups

MATERIALS AND SUPPLIES

Flat buttons and poker chips
Posterboard
Butcher paper
Tape
Crayons with the paper removed

Let the children help you spread the buttons and chips on the table/floor or make *"Button Boards"* by gluing the buttons and chips on large pieces of posterboard. Cover the chips with a piece of butcher paper. Tape the corners of the paper down. Put a container of crayons near the paper.

ACTIVITY

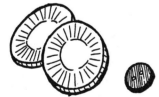

Let the children choose crayons and lie on their stomachs around the edges of the paper. Have the children use their hands to feel around on top of the paper to locate the objects, and then rub their crayons over them so that the outlines appear. Continue feeling and coloring until all of the objects have been discovered and colored. Hang the **Button Rub** on the wall for everyone to see.

VARIATIONS:

Shape Rub: Cut out large posterboard shapes, letters, and/or numbers. Put them under the paper and do more rubbings.

Two Color Rub: Put only two colors of crayons out with poker chips and bingo chips under the paper. Have the children use one color to rub over the larger chips and the other color to rub the smaller chips.

Starlight: Use black paper and white crayons. Try it with your eyes closed or while wearing dark sun glasses.

Get A Glove

CHILDREN WILL DEVELOP	USE WITH:
Tactile Awareness	Small groups
Body Awareness	Large groups

MATERIALS AND SUPPLIES

As many different types of gloves and mittens as possible -- at least one pair for each child plus several extras. (Duplicates are OK.)

Rubber gloves	Leather work gloves
Winter gloves	Cotton gloves
Boxing gloves	Oven mittens
Baseball gloves	Winter mittens

ACTIVITY

Have the children stand or sit in a circle. Put all of the gloves/mittens in the middle so that the children can easily see them. Let each child choose a pair of gloves or mittens to put on. While the children are wearing the mittens/gloves, give them verbal and/or non-verbal commands such as:

- Touch your head.
- Touch your knees.
- Shake your neighbor's hand.
- Clap your hands.

After several commands, have the children take off their gloves/mittens, pass them to their neighbors and then put on the new pairs. Continue playing until everyone has experienced many different gloves and mittens.

VARIATIONS:

Hot Potato: Have a variety of objects such as a doll, a fabric ball, a block, etc. in a box. Take out an object and play *"Hot Potato"* with it while the children are wearing the gloves. Change objects and play again.

Salt Trays

CHILDREN WILL DEVELOP	USE WITH:
Arm, Hand, Finger Coordination	Individuals
Eye-Hand Coordination	Small groups
Tactile Discrimination	

MATERIALS AND SUPPLIES

Brownie pans
Salt
Adhesive paper or wallpaper

Cover the bottom of each pan with brightly colored adhesive paper or wallpaper. Pour a half inch of salt in each.

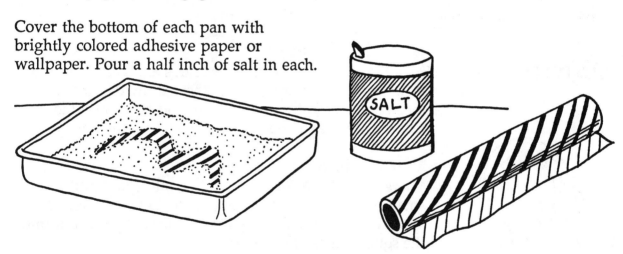

ACTIVITY   Let the children write or draw designs, pictures, shapes, letters, numbers, etc. with a particular finger, an elbow, or a toe. Jiggle the pan to erase the drawings and draw again and again using the same or a different body part.

VARIATIONS:

Trying Textures: Put a variety of materials, such as baking soda, corn starch, or sand in different trays so that the children can feel and compare the textures.

More Texture Drawing: Put out a container with a narrow paint brush, wooden dowel rod, unsharpened pencil, Q-Tip, and typewriter eraser. Let the children use the different *"tools"* to write and draw in the salt trays.

Carpet Caper

CHILDREN WILL DEVELOP
    Tactile Awareness
    Eye-Hand Coordination
    Visual Motor Control

USE WITH:
    Individuals
    Small groups

MATERIALS AND SUPPLIES

Carpet squares
Chalk

Have carpet squares available.

ACTIVITY

Have the children take carpet squares and chalk and put them on the table or floor. Let them draw designs, pictures, letters, etc. on the carpet and then erase the marks with their hands, elbows, and/or bare feet.

VARIATIONS:

Where Did It Go? Pour corn starch into spice bottles with small holes and put them on a table. Let the children sprinkle corn starch on the carpet squares and rub it into the squares until it disappears.

HINT: Cover some of the holes with tape if too much corn starch comes out at one time.

Sticker Stick-Ons

CHILDREN WILL DEVELOP
Tactile Discrimination
Arm, Hand, Finger Coordination

USE WITH:
Individuals
Small groups

MATERIALS AND SUPPLIES

Removable dot stickers
Smelly stickers
Small container
Waxed paper

Put 5 - 10 stickers on sheets of
waxed paper. Put the sheets in
a small container.

ACTIVITY

Let each child pick his own sheet of stickers and then
randomly place the individual stickers up, down, and all
around one of his arms. Have each child close his eyes
and then feel, find, and remove the stickers one at a time,
putting each one on his piece of waxed paper. Play again
and again using the same and/or different stickers.

VARIATIONS:

Smells Like ... : Have one child close his eyes. Place
several different smelly stickers on one or both arms. Ask
him to find a sticker, take it off, smell it, and tell
you/other children what it smells like.

Where's The Raspberry? This time have the child smell the
stickers on his arms until he finds a specific scent. When
he does, let him remove it and put it on a piece of waxed
paper.

Yarn Cocoon

MATERIALS AND SUPPLIES

Several balls of yarn

Each pair of children will need one ball of yarn.

ACTIVITY

Play **Yarn Cocoon** in pairs. One child stands with his arms held snugly around the front of his waist, holding onto one end of the ball of yarn. The partner wraps the yarn around the first child's legs or upper body, thus making a yarn cocoon. After the cocoon is finished, the second child slowly unwraps the yarn from around the first child's legs or upper body, winding it back up into a ball as she goes. Now change places and make another cocoon.

VARIATIONS:

Whole Body Cocoons: Let the children wrap each other in **Whole Body Yarn Cocoons** starting at the shoulders and ending at the ankles. (Remember safety.)

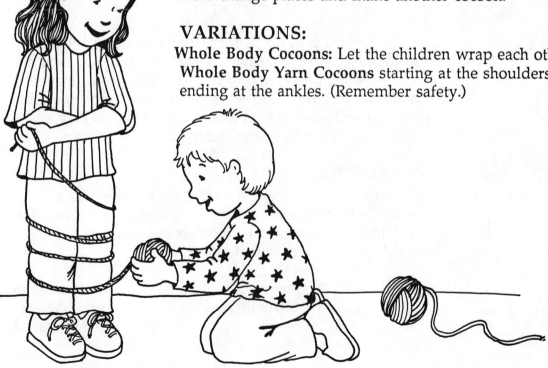

26

Cotton In The Dark

CHILDREN WILL DEVELOP
Tactile Discrimination
Position In Space
Motor Planning

USE WITH:
Individuals
Small groups

MATERIALS AND SUPPLIES

Cotton balls
Small containers

Put the cotton balls in a container.
Set them on the floor. Have a stack
of 3-5 small containers.

ACTIVITY

Ask the children to help you spread the cotton balls
randomly on the floor or table. Have each child close his
eyes or wear sunglasses and crawl around on his hands
and knees, feeling for and finding the cotton balls. When
he finds a ball he should open his eyes and put it in a
container, then close his eyes and continue the search.

VARIATIONS:

In Pairs: Play this game in pairs with one child holding
the container and the other child searching for the cotton
balls. After a while switch.

In the Dark Again: Use pom-poms, sponges, feathers,
Nerf balls, or ping pong balls instead of cotton balls.

Stencil Fingerpainting

CHILDREN WILL DEVELOP
Tactile Awareness
Finger Coordination
Visual Motor Coordination

USE WITH:
Individuals
Small groups

MATERIALS AND SUPPLIES

Fingerpaint   Construction paper
Plastic stencils   Paper towels
Coffee can lids   Small containers
Meat trays   Plastic spoons

Cut 8 - 10 stencils out of coffee can lids or styrofoam meat trays. Tape some of the stencils to pieces of construction paper and others to the top of a table. Have several small containers of fingerpaint near the stencils.

ACTIVITY

Let each child choose whether she wants to stencil paint on construction paper or the table. Then let her spoon fingerpaint inside her stencil and use her finger to spread it around until the whole inside area is covered. After each child is finished have her wash her hands or wipe them off with paper towels.

NOTE: Encourage the children to use only one finger to spread the fingerpaint.

VARIATIONS:

Jelly Stenciling: Use petroleum jelly instead of fingerpaint and waxed paper instead of construction paper.

Stencil Murals: Cover the table with butcher paper and stencil all over it. Hang your mural on a wall or bulletin board.

28

Pinch Of Playdough

CHILDREN WILL DEVELOP
Tactile Discrimination
Finger Coordination

USE WITH:
Individuals
Small groups

MATERIALS AND SUPPLIES

Playdough
Bingo chips
A large and small container

Make a giant batch of playdough with the children and hide the chips inside of it. Put the dough and containers on the table.

ACTIVITY

Let the children pinch off small pieces of playdough from the giant piece. While they are pinching the playdough, have them search for chips. When they find a chip have them clean it off and put it in the small container and put the excess playdough in the large container. After all of the chips have been found, roll all of the *"pinches"* back into a giant piece. Hide the chips and play again.

NOTE: Encourage the children to *"pinch the playdough"* with their forefingers and thumbs.

VARIATIONS:
Treasure Hunt: Hide buttons, beads, rubber eraser figures, etc. inside the playdough.

Texture Bag

CHILDREN WILL DEVELOP
  Tactile Discrimination
  Hand Control
  Body Awareness

USE WITH:
  Small groups
  Large groups

MATERIALS AND SUPPLIES

Record/tape player
A large bag such as a pillow case
Variety of objects (at least one for each child):

Soft brush	Piece of lamb's wool	Variety of fabric
Feather duster	Sea sponge	velvet
Rubber glove	Paint roller	satin
Scouring pad	Paint brush	burlap
Piece of fur		

Put the objects in the bag.

ACTIVITY

Have the children sit in a large circle, remove their shoes and socks, and roll up their pant legs. Walk around with the **Texture Bag** and let each child select an item from the bag. After each child has an object, start the music. While the music is playing, encourage the children to feel their items and to rub them on their face, hands, arms, feet and legs. Stop the music and talk about how the items felt - soft, scratchy, rough, etc. Have each child pass his item to the person sitting next to him. Continue playing until the children have experienced many of the textures.

Soap Crayons

CHILDREN WILL DEVELOP
    Tactile Discrimination
    Eye-Hand Coordination
    Body Awareness

USE WITH:
    Individuals
    Small groups

MATERIALS AND SUPPLIES

Different colored soap crayons
Sponges
Containers

Cut the sponges into 2"x2" pieces and put them in a container. Pour water into several other containers. Set the sponges, water, and soap crayons on the table.

ACTIVITY

Allow the children to freely explore the soap crayons by drawing and writing on their arms and hands. When they are finished, let them use the small sponges and water to wash off their lines and drawings.

VARIATIONS:

Line Up: Have the children draw lines from each of their fingertips to their elbows using a different color for each line. Let them do one or both sides of their hands and arms. After they have drawn their lines, encourage them to wash off one line at a time using the small sponges.

31

Finger Licking Snack

CHILDREN WILL DEVELOP
   Finger Coordination
   Tactile Discrimination
   Eye-Hand Coordination

USE WITH:
   Individuals
   Small groups

MATERIALS AND SUPPLIES

Cereal, such as
   Cheerios
Peanut butter

Small plates
Napkins
Spoons/scoops

Put the cereal and peanut butter in small containers. Put scoops with the cereal and spoons with the peanut butter.

ACTIVITY

Have the children wash their hands and then get a plate. Pass the peanut butter and let each child spoon some on her plate; then pass the cereal and let each child scoop that on her plate.

Have each child stick one finger at a time into the peanut butter and then pick up the cereal by touching her peanut butter fingertip to a piece of cereal. Tell the children to eat the snack one finger at a time.

VARIATIONS:

Raisins And Cream Cheese: Use raisins instead of cereal and/or cream cheese instead of peanut butter.

One-To-One Snack: Have the children dab peanut butter on each of their fingers by sticking one fingertip at a time into the peanut butter. Have them touch each fingertip to separate pieces of cereal, trying not to let their tips touch. After all of the fingertips have a piece of cereal on them, eat the snack one finger at a time.

Finger Spread

CHILDREN WILL DEVELOP
- Tactile Discrimination
- Eye-Hand Coordination
- Finger Coordination

USE WITH:
- Individuals
- Small groups
- Large groups

MATERIALS AND SUPPLIES

Spoons
Small plates or bowls
Napkins

Breads:
- Bagels
- Graham crackers
- Saltine crackers

Toppings:
- Cream cheese
- Soft cheese
- Peanut butter
- Fruit spread
- Honey

Put each type of food and a spoon on a plate or in a bowl.

ACTIVITY

Have the children wash their hands and then take a plate and napkin. Pass the bread and toppings. Let each child spoon a little of each topping on his plate and then, using one index finger, spread each topping on his bread. After the children have spread their toppings have them wipe their fingers with their napkins and then enjoy the special snack with a drink.

Gooey Bags

CHILDREN WILL DEVELOP
Hand Strength
Tactile Discrimination
Eye-Hand Coordination

USE WITH:
Individuals
Small groups

MATERIALS AND SUPPLIES

Small containers
Resealable plastic bags
Masking tape
Spoons

Mixers:
Corn starch
Salt
Styrofoam peanuts
Shaving cream

Bird seed
Water
Several colors of fingerpaint

Stack the plastic bags on a tray. Put the *"mixers"* in separate containers with spoons. Place all of the containers on a table or low counter.

ACTIVITY

Let the children spoon small amounts of the different mixers into their bags. After a child has filled his bag with whatever combination he wants, help him lay it flat on the table and remove the excess air. Seal each bag, tape it closed, and write the child's name on it.

Sit with the children as they squeeze and press their bags to mix up all of the materials. Encourage them to:

- Observe how their mixtures are changing colors and consistency.
- Talk about and describe how their mixtures look and feel.

VARIATIONS:

Spoon Out: Offer the children a variety of tools such as soup ladles, eye droppers, ice tongs, forks, spoons etc. to *spoon out* the different mixers.

Goop

MATERIALS AND SUPPLIES

Corn starch   Large cake/ brownie pans or trays
Water   1 cup measuring scoop

Put the corn starch, a container of water, and a tray on the table.

ACTIVITY   Put about one cup of corn starch on a tray. Slowly pour water on the tray while a child mixes the corn starch and water with her hands. Continue adding water until the *Goop* mixture is the consistency of white glue.

Allow the children lots of time to explore the *Goop* on the tray. Encourage them to gather it into their hands and let it run through their fingers. What happens to it? How does it feel?

VARIATIONS:
Warm And Cold Goop: Use water of different temperatures.

Colored Goop: Add food coloring.

Eyedropper Goop: Have the children add water to the corn starch using eye droppers.

Texture Goop: Add textures such as rice, sand, and bird seed.

Outside Goop: On a warm day, use ice cubes instead of water.

Feely Bags

CHILDREN WILL DEVELOP
Tactile Discrimination
Arm, Hand, Finger Coordination
Visual Memory

USE WITH:
Small groups
Large groups

MATERIALS AND SUPPLIES

Brown paper lunch bags

Have the children sit in a group. Give each child a bag.

ACTIVITY

Count together "1,2,3." Have the children get up, walk around the classroom to find an object. After each child finds one, she should secretly slip it into her bag and tiptoe back to the group.

After the children are back, have them close their bags and pass them to their neighbors. Each child should then slip her hand into the bag, feel the object, and try to figure out what it is. Let a child tell her guess if she wants and then take the object out for everyone to see. Clap! Let another child share his guess. Continue in this manner until everyone has shown the group what is in his bag.

Count "1,2,3" and then everyone gets up and puts her object back in its place in the classroom.

Little Hand Mixers

CHILDREN WILL DEVELOP
Hand Strength
Hand Coordination
Tactile Awareness

USE WITH:
Individuals
Small groups

MATERIALS AND SUPPLIES

Corn muffin mix and ingredients
Large resealable plastic bag
Muffin pan

Put all of the ingredients on the table.

ACTIVITY

Have everyone wash his hands. Follow the directions on the package, except have the children put the ingredients in the resealable bag, instead of a bowl. Push, poke, and mix the ingredients around in the bag. Empty the mixture into a muffin pan and bake. Enjoy warm corn muffins with a drink.

VARIATIONS:

More Cooking: Use the same procedure when mixing pancakes, cookies, and easy breads.

Skin Sensations

CHILDREN WILL DEVELOP
Tactile Discrimination
Eye-Hand Coordination
Body Awareness

USE WITH:
Individuals
Small groups

MATERIALS AND SUPPLIES

Tray	Applicators	Sheep skin
Body Lotion	Cotton balls	Small paint rollers
Corn starch	Paint brushes	Loofa sponges
Shaving cream	Q-Tips	Burlap
Powder without talc	Sponges	Popsicle sticks

Have the lotions, powders, creams, and applicators on a tray.

ACTIVITY

Let each child choose a lotion, powder, or cream. Use one of the applicators to apply it to his hands, arms, legs, and/or feet. Each child can rub it into his skin. Apply some more if the child wants and let him rub again.

VARIATIONS:

Hand Massager: Use a hand held massager to apply the lotion or shaving cream.

Popsicle Stick Shaving: Use a popsicle stick to *shave off* the shaving cream.

I'll Do It Myself: After the children are familiar with the materials and procedure, allow them to use a variety of applicators. Be sure to have a waste basket nearby to throw away the used applicators.

38

Silly Putty

MATERIALS AND SUPPLIES

White glue
Blue liquid starch
Large bowl

Measure one cup of white glue and a cup of starch.

ACTIVITY

Mix the **Silly Putty** by pouring the white glue and liquid starch into a bowl and mixing the ingredients together. Add more glue if the mixture is too thin or more starch if the mixture is too sticky. Store the **Silly Putty** in a covered air-tight container at room temperature.

Let the children freely explore the **Silly Putty**. Encourage them to form it, roll it, stretch it, pull it apart, or cut it with scissors and dull knives.

VARIATIONS:

Colored Putty: Add food coloring.

Smelly Putty: Add scents

Single Putty: Help each child make an individual portion of putty in a small bowl or cup. Put it in a sandwich bag to take home and enjoy.

Fingerpainting Fun

CHILDREN WILL DEVELOP
Finger Coordination
Tactile Awareness
Eye-Hand Coordination

USE WITH:
Individuals
Small groups

MATERIALS AND SUPPLIES

Fingerpaints
Shaving Cream
Hand lotion
Liquid soap
Petroleum jelly
Fingerpaints
Ivory Snow powder

Paint On
Paper Plates
Trays
Aluminum foil
Table tops
Meat trays
Sandpaper
Corrugated paper
Plastic bubble packing

Materials To Add
Food coloring
Scents
Coffee grounds
Sand
Aquarium gravel
Saw dust

Choose the materials and supplies you need for the activity and put them in the designated area.

ACTIVITY

Allow the children sufficient time to explore the painting material before adding any extra materials or textures.

VARIATIONS:
Use Different Body Parts
- Hands ● Fingernails
- Elbow ● One finger

Fingerpaint In Different Positions
- Sitting at a table
- Standing at a table
- Standing with paper tapped to a wall or clipped to an easel
- Lying on their stomachs with the paper on the floor
- Lying on their backs with the paper taped to the underside of a table

Hand Lotion Massage

CHILDREN WILL DEVELOP
Tactile Awareness
Hand Strength
Hand Coordination

USE WITH:
Individuals
Small groups
Large groups

MATERIALS AND SUPPLIES

Several bottles of hand lotion

Set the bottles of hand lotion on different high shelves around the room.

ACTIVITY

Hand Massage - Give each child a small amount of lotion and then have him vigorously rub his hands together using a lot of pressure.

Finger Massage - Have each child take hold of one finger with his opposite hand, squeeze it, and then pull the finger out using a downward pulling motion. Massage each finger in this way.

NOTE: This is a good exercise to do before any drawing, cutting, or writing activity.

Floating Icebergs

CHILDREN WILL DEVELOP
Tactile Discrimination
Finger Coordination
Hand Coordination

USE WITH:
Individuals

MATERIALS AND SUPPLIES

Dish tub or water table
Lots of ice cubes
Several small buckets, preferably with handles
Beach towel

Put the beach towel under the water table or dish tub. Add water to your water table and dump one or two trays of ice cubes in the table/tub. Put small buckets nearby.

ACTIVITY   Have a child get a small bucket and stand by the water
table/tub. Wearing sunglasses or closing her eyes and
holding the bucket in one hand, let her feel in the water
for the ice cubes, grab them, and put them in the bucket.
After she has finished, she can dump the ice cubes back
into the water to play again or to
prepare the game for other children.
(Add ice cubes as they melt.)

VARIATIONS:

Colored Cubes: Have two buckets. Make
clear and colored cubes. Float both in the
water. Using their hands, have the
children catch the cubes putting the
colored cubes in one bucket and the
clear cubes in the other bucket.

Only The Ice: Float
other objects with the
ice cubes but have
the children pick
out only the ice
cubes.

42

Spray And Wipe

CHILDREN WILL DEVELOP
Hand Strength
Eye-Hand Coordination
Body Awareness

USE WITH:
Small groups

MATERIALS AND SUPPLIES

Water
Spray bottles
Variety of wiping materials:
Cloths
Paper towels
Sponges

Fill the spray bottles with slightly warm water.

ACTIVITY

Play **Spray And Wipe** with partners sitting on the floor or in a sunny place outside. One child takes off his shoes and socks, rolls up his pant legs, closes his eyes, and holds the wiping materials in his lap. The other child has a spray bottle. She sprays water on one of her partner's hands, legs, feet, or arms. Each time the first child is sprayed, he wipes the water off with one of the wiping materials. After several **Spray And Wipes**, the children change places.

VARIATIONS:

Different Temperatures: Fill the spray bottles with reasonably different temperatures of water. Let the children use two or three bottles at a time.

Clip-Ons

CHILDREN WILL DEVELOP
Tactile Discrimination
Finger Coordination
Hand Coordination

USE WITH:
Small groups

MATERIALS AND SUPPLIES

Variety of clips:
Butterfly
Hair
Metal Office

Spring clothespins
Snack bag clips

Put the clips in a container. Set the container on a table or shelf.

ACTIVITY

Play **Clip-Ons** in pairs. One child closes her eyes and the other child randomly places the clips on the first child's clothing. After all of the clips are on, the first child feels around her clothes, finds the clips, and removes them before opening her eyes. Clap! The children change roles and play again.

What's Under The Blanket?

CHILDREN WILL DEVELOP
  Tactile Discrimination
  Visual Memory
  Hand Coordination

USE WITH:
  Small groups
  Large groups

MATERIALS AND SUPPLIES

Large, thin blanket or sheet
Variety of familiar objects, such as: toys, shoes, stapler, ruler, and book

While the children are out of the room, spread the objects on the floor and cover them with the blanket.

ACTIVITY

Have the children sit around the blanket. While keeping the objects covered, encourage the children to use their hands to feel the objects through the blanket. Tell them to think about what the hidden objects are. They should keep their guesses to themselves.

After the children have had sufficient time to explore and feel the objects, let the children call out their guesses. List the guesses on a sheet of paper. Read the list to the children. Uncover the objects and discover the true identity of all those lumps.

Stay On The Glue Road

CHILDREN WILL DEVELOP
Tactile Discrimination
Arm, Hand, Finger Coordination
Visual Motor Coordination

USE WITH:
Individuals
Small groups

MATERIALS AND SUPPLIES

Large sheet of tagboard/posterboard
White glue colored with food coloring

Construct glue roads. To make each road, slowly drizzle a single continuous line of glue from one edge of the posterboard to the other. Be certain to include curves and zig-zags. Make different roads on other pieces of posterboard.

ACTIVITY

Put the board/s on the table or floor. Let the children pretend that their fingers are cars. *Drive* the *cars* along the different roads.

VARIATIONS:

Up and Down and All Around Roads: Make several roads of different colors on one piece of posterboard.

Car Rides: Have the children drive small vehicles on the roads. (Add houses, etc. for dramatic play.)

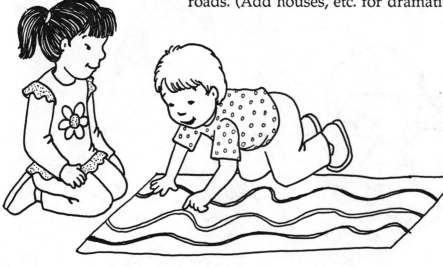

Close Your Eyes: Have the children close their eyes and *drive* down the roads with their fingers.

Index-Finger Cars: Encourage the children to *drive* down the roads with only their index fingers.

46

Rub A Dub

CHILDREN WILL DEVELOP
    Hand Strength
    Hand Coordination
    Visual Motor Control

USE WITH:
    Individuals
    Small groups

MATERIALS AND SUPPLIES

Wash tub/water table   Small buckets
Doll clothes   Clothesline
Washcloths   Clothespins

Fill the tub/water table with warm water. Put the doll clothes and washcloths in a bucket and the clothespins in a small container. Hang up the clothesline. Lay a beach towel under the clothesline.

ACTIVITY

Have the children wash the items, getting them very wet. Tell them to squeeze and wring out the items until most of the water is removed. Allow the children to rewash and wring out as often as they would like. Then the children can clip the items to the clothesline to finish drying.

VARIATIONS:

In The Wash Tub: If you think that it is too difficult for your children to clip the clothes with clothespins, let them wring out the items and put them in a wash tub rather than hanging them on the clothesline.

Rubber Fingers

CHILDREN WILL DEVELOP
    Hand Strength
    Hand Coordination
    Eye-Hand Coordination

USE WITH:
    Small groups

MATERIALS AND SUPPLIES

One package of colored rubber bands

Put the rubber bands in a container. Set the container on the table.

ACTIVITY

Play **Rubber Fingers** in pairs. Have the children sit facing each other. One child has the container of rubber bands; the other child holds up one hand in front of her with her fingers spread apart. The child with the rubber bands stretches them on her partner's hand from each of her fingers to her thumb.

    After the rubber bands are on, encourage both children to say and do the motions to *Open Them, Shut Them.* After saying the rhyme, take off the rubber bands, one at a time, always lifting off the top one next. The children can change places and play **Rubber Fingers** again.

VARIATIONS:
Two Hands: Using both hands, stretch rubber bands from the fingers of one hand to those on the other one.

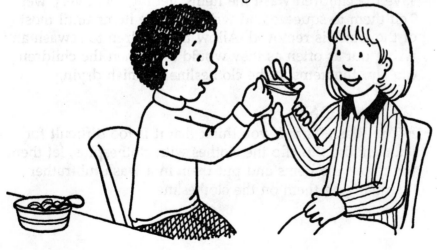

Crush And Crumple

CHILDREN WILL DEVELOP
Hand Strength
Hand Coordination
Eye-Hand Coordination

USE WITH:
Individuals
Small groups

MATERIALS AND SUPPLIES

Full pages of newspaper
Large box
Sheet

Tear each sheet of newspaper into four pieces. (Younger children need smaller pieces.) Put the pile of newspaper pieces near the large box.

ACTIVITY

Have the children use two hands to crumple each piece of newspaper into a small, tight ball. Put the balls in a box. The children can:
- Toss them into a bucket while standing or lying on their stomachs.
- Make a mountain and crawl through it.
- Hold onto the edge of the sheet and shake the balls to make *popcorn*.
- Stuff them into old child or adult-size clothing to make dolls. Use a stuffed paper sack for the head.

VARIATIONS:

More Muscle: To offer more resistance use cardboard rolls from toilet paper and paper towels. Let the children crush them using one or two hands.

Behind The Back: *Challenge* the children to crumple the paper with one hand while keeping their other hand behind their backs.

Sponge Squeeze

CHILDREN WILL DEVELOP
Hand Strength
Hand Coordination
Eye-Hand Coordination

USE WITH:
Individuals
Small groups

MATERIALS AND SUPPLIES

Sponges
Several margarine tubs
Beach towel

Cut the sponges into 2"x2" pieces. Fill several margarine tubs about half full of water. Lay the beach towel on the table or floor. Put the containers on top of the towel.

ACTIVITY

Give each child one empty tub and one filled with water. Let him dip his sponge into the water and then squeeze the water out into the empty container. Let him continue until all of the water has been squeezed out of one container into the other one. If the child would like, he can reverse and squeeze the water back into the first tub.

VARIATIONS:

Finger Squeeze: Have the children use only their thumb and first two fingers to squeeze the water out of the sponges.

Big Squeeze: Have one large dish tub filled with water on the table. Give each child an empty container. Use larger sponges or foam balls for more hand strength.

Colored Water: Add food coloring to the water.

Smelly Water: Add scents to the water.

Spray Bottle Fun

CHILDREN WILL DEVELOP
- Hand Strength
- Eye-Hand Coordination
- Visual Motor Control

USE WITH:
- Individuals
- Small groups

MATERIALS AND SUPPLIES

Buckets   Food coloring
Spray bottles   White bed sheet/white fabric
Water

Fill spray bottles with colored water. Lay the bed sheet/fabric on the floor. Put the bottles nearby.

ACTIVITY

Have the children spray the bed sheet/fabric with colored water. Let the fabric dry. Hang the *"Colored Water Mural"* on a large empty wall.

VARIATIONS:

Spray The Bushes: Take the spray bottles and buckets of clear water outside. Let the children spray the bushes, sidewalks, play equipment, trees. etc. Refill the bottles with the water from the buckets.

Water The Plants: Have the children use spray bottles to water the plants in the classroom.

Moisten The Sand: Have several spray bottles in the sand table. Children can moisten the sand as they build, mold, tunnel, and poke.

Playdough Exercises

CHILDREN WILL DEVELOP
Hand Strength
Hand Coordination
Finger Coordination

USE WITH:
Individuals
Small groups
Large groups

MATERIALS AND SUPPLIES

Playdough

ACTIVITY
Do playdough exercises with the children while sitting at the art table.

VARIATIONS:

Copy Cat: Demonstrate an exercise and have the children copy you. Remember to give them ample time to practice each exercise before doing another one. No hurry.

- Squeeze and release the ball of playdough while holding it palm up. Repeat with the same or other hand.

- Roll the ball of playdough between both hands with one palm up and one palm down.

- Roll a ball of playdough around and around on the table with one hand. Say *"Round and round..."* as you roll.

- Flatten the ball of playdough by pounding it with the side of a fist. Try the other fist.

- Flatten the ball of playdough with the side of an open hand. Try the other hand.

- Form a *mountain* by placing your hand over the flattened playdough and slowly closing it, drawing the playdough up into your palm.

- Make the ball of playdough into a snake by rolling it on the table using one hand, two hands, or between both hands off the table.

- Using the thumb and forefinger of one or both hands, pinch off small pieces of the ball, snake, or mountain of playdough, until it's all pinched apart. Pick up the pinched parts by dabbing them back together again and forming a giant ball.

- Flatten the playdough ball by pounding it with the palm of an open hand. *"You're making it so flat."*

Cotton Ball Road Rally

> **CHILDREN WILL DEVELOP**
> Hand Strength
> Eye-Hand Coordination
> Motor Planning
>
> **USE WITH:**
> Individuals
> Small groups

MATERIALS AND SUPPLIES

Masking tape
Scooter boards
Several containers

Cotton balls or ping-pong balls
Plastic squeeze containers, such as those
   used for ketchup or mustard

Tape a straight line on the floor to make a road. Put the balls in a container. Set the containers, squeeze bottles, and scooter boards near the tape.

ACTIVITY

Let each child get on a scooter board and take a cotton ball and a squeeze bottle. Have him put his ball on the road and *drive* it along by blowing it with the squeeze bottle.

NOTE: Encourage the children to do this activity in a variety of positions:
- Sitting on a scooter board
- Kneeling on a scooter board
- Lying on a scooter board
- Lying on the floor

VARIATIONS:

Zig-Zag Drive: As the children become proficient at this activity, change the line to an 'S' curve or *zig-zag* line; add tunnels, etc.

Turkey Baster Blasters

CHILDREN WILL DEVELOP
- Hand Strength
- Eye-Hand Coordination
- Visual Motor Control

USE WITH:
- Individuals
- Small groups

MATERIALS AND SUPPLIES

Turkey basters
Small plastic swimming pool
Small margarine tubs

Fill the swimming pool with water. Float the margarine tubs in the pool. Put the turkey basters nearby.

ACTIVITY

Let the children lie down next to the pool. Each child fills his baster with water from the pool and then squirts it into one of the floating containers. Continue until the containers are full and have sunk. Dump the water back into the swimming pool and play again.

VARIATIONS:

Water Table Fun: Fill the water table, float the empty containers, and let the children play **Turkey Baster Blasters** while standing around the table.

Kooky Cut-Ups

MATERIALS AND SUPPLIES
Scissors
Materials to cut:

Yarn	Tagboard	Brown grocery bags
Twine	Styrofoam meat trays	Cereal boxes
Straws	Packing peanuts	Thin packing foam
Corrugated cardboard	Lightweight cardboard	Waxed paper

Put several different materials, scissors, and your collage box or small boxes such as shoe boxes on the art table.

ACTIVITY

Let the children cut the materials into small pieces and put them into the collage box. Use these materials for gluing and pasting activities. Repeat often using a new variety of materials each time.

NOTE: Before children begin formal cutting projects, let them have a lot of experience and practice cutting a variety of materials to develop their cutting skills.

VARIATIONS:
Dough Cut: Offer scissors with clay, playdough, and silly putty.

Hand Warm-Ups

CHILDREN WILL DEVELOP
Hand Strength
Hand Control
Hand Coordination

USE WITH:
Individuals
Small groups
Large groups

MATERIALS AND SUPPLIES
Tennis balls
Nerf balls
Rubber hand exercisers
Socks rolled into balls
Thick rectangles of foam rubber

Put the items in a box.

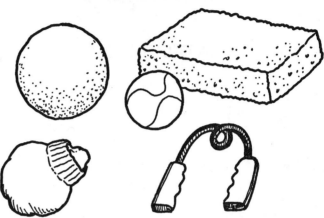

ACTIVITY

Before any cutting, drawing or writing activity, have the children exercise their hands for several minutes by squeezing and releasing the materials with one or both hands.

Water Balloon Fun

CHILDREN WILL DEVELOP
Hand Strength
Hand Control
Hand Coordination

USE WITH:
Individuals
Small groups
Large groups

MATERIALS AND SUPPLIES

Extra-firm balloons in a variety of shapes and sizes,
   such as inflatable punch balls
Water table

Partially fill 4 to 6 balloons with water and tie the ends. Put the balloons in the water table.

ACTIVITY

Let the children manipulate the balloons* in their hands by squeezing them, rolling them around, holding and shaking them, squeezing them together with their palms, and rolling them in the water table. Encourage the children to exchange balloons and experience a variety of sizes and shapes.

VARIATIONS:

Hot and Cold Balloons: Fill half of the balloons with very cold water and the rest with warm water.

Remember Safety: Be sure to use extra-firm balloons, such as inflatable punch balls. Monitor the activity at all times. If a balloon should break remove it immediately.

Hand Mixed Cookies

CHILDREN WILL DEVELOP
Hand Strength
Hand Coordination
Visual Motor Control

USE WITH:
Individuals
Small groups
Large groups

MATERIALS AND SUPPLIES

Large resealable plastic bag
Cookie sheet
Measuring cups
Food items for your children's favorite cookie recipe

Put the food items and utensils on the table

ACTIVITY

Have all of the children wash their hands. Read the recipe aloud. As you do let the children help you measure the food items and put them in the resealable bag.

After all of the items are in the bag, seal it up. Pass the bag around and let the children mix, mash, knead, and pound the dough with their hands.

Open the bag, give each child some dough, and let him form it into small balls. Bake the cookies according to the directions.

Line Punching

CHILDREN WILL DEVELOP
Hand Strength
Hand Coordination
Eye-Hand Coordination

USE WITH:
Individuals
Small groups

MATERIALS AND SUPPLIES

Hand-held hole punches
Adding machine tape
Crayons and/or markers

Cut the adding machine tape into 12 inch strips. Have the strips of paper, hole punches, crayons, and/or markers on the table.

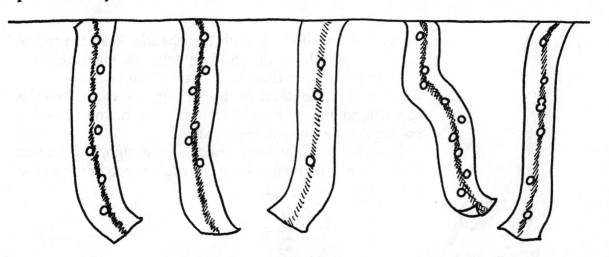

ACTIVITY

Have each child draw a line across the middle of the paper from one end to the other. Put a big dot on the left end. Beginning at the left side (by the dot) of the paper, encourage the child to punch as many holes as he would like on the line. Hang the **Line Punches** from your ceiling.

VARIATIONS:

Punch Alongs: Instead of drawing a line, let the children punch holes anywhere they like on their strips of paper.

Muscles: Use thicker paper to provide more resistance.

Pretzel Put-Ons

CHILDREN WILL DEVELOP
Finger Coordination
Eye-Hand Coordination
Visual Motor Control

USE WITH:
Individuals
Small groups
Large groups

MATERIALS AND SUPPLIES

Thick pretzel sticks
Peanut butter
Raisins
Small pieces of cereal
Paper plates

Have pretzels, peanut butter, raisins, and
cereals in different containers.

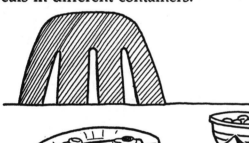

ACTIVITY

Have all of the children wash their hands and then take
plates. Pass the food items and let the children put some of
each on their plates. Let the children use one of their index
fingers to spread the peanut butter on their pretzels and
then have them put raisins and cereal bits on the peanut
butter. Eat and enjoy with a glass of milk, water, or juice.

VARIATIONS:

Dab The Peanut Butter: Allow the children to dab peanut
butter on the pretzel sticks and then put one food item on
each dab.

61

Finger Weaving

CHILDREN WILL DEVELOP
Hand Coordination
Finger Coordination
Eye-Hand Coordination

USE WITH:
Individuals
Small groups
Large groups

MATERIALS AND SUPPLIES

Hangers
Yarn

Cut the yarn into three foot lengths.
Tie a loop at one end of each piece.
Clip them to a hanger.

ACTIVITY

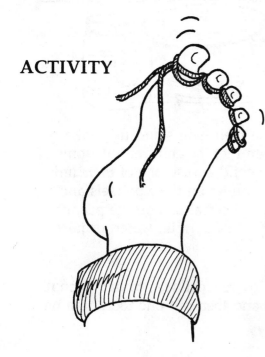

Have a child unclip a piece of yarn, slip the loop over one thumb to secure it and then begin to weave the yarn in and out between his fingers until all of the yarn is used up. Now let him unweave the piece of yarn. Repeat **Finger Weaving** on that hand or the other one. When finished clip the yarn back onto the hanger.

VARIATIONS:

More Finger Weaving: Use ribbons, elastic, string, and a variety of textures of yarn.

Toe Weaving: Let the children weave the yarn, string, etc. around and between their toes.

Food Sculptures

CHILDREN WILL DEVELOP
Finger Coordination
Eye-Hand Coordination
Visual Motor Control

USE WITH:
Individuals
Small groups

MATERIALS AND SUPPLIES

Snack foods:
Thin pretzel sticks   Graham crackers
Peanut butter   Raisins
Dry cereal   Cream cheese
Sandwich bags
Paper plates

Have the different food items in separate containers. Put the food and the plates on the table.

ACTIVITY

Have the children wash their hands and then get plates. Using the peanut butter and/or cream cheese for adhesives and the graham crackers as a base, let the children use the food items to build **Food Sculptures**. Encourage them to build their sculptures out as well as up. When each child has finished building his snack, let him eat it with a drink.

NOTE: Instead of eating the snack right away, let each child put it on a plate and slip it into a sandwich bag for later. (Write each child's name on a piece of tape and put it on his bag.) At snack, pass out the sculptures and enjoy with drinks.

Wacky Wires

CHILDREN WILL DEVELOP
    Finger Coordination
    Eye-Hand Coordination
    Visual Motor Control

USE WITH:
    Individuals
    Small groups

MATERIALS AND SUPPLIES

Pieces of coated electrical or telephone wire

Put the pieces of wire on a tray or in a shallow box.

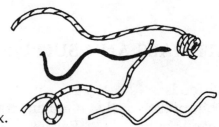

ACTIVITY

Set the container of wire pieces on a table or on the floor. Let the children bend, twist, squeeze, connect, and explore the wire. Before putting them away, have the children straighten all of the pieces of wire to provide additional development of their dexterity and coordination.

VARIATIONS:

Copy Cat Designs: Have the children work in pairs. Have one child copy the wire pattern or design of her partner. Let the children switch roles and play **Copy Cat Designs** again.

Tweezers And Beads

MATERIALS AND SUPPLIES

Trays
Small tweezers
Small beads
Rubber, suction cup soap holders
Margarine containers

Put beads in small containers. On each of several trays, put a container of beads, tweezers, and soap dish. Put the trays on the table.

ACTIVITY

Let the children use tweezers to pick up the beads and place them on the suction cups of the soap holders. Continue playing until all of the suction cups are filled. Reverse the game and put the beads back in the container. Play again and again.

VARIATIONS:

Tweezers and Toothpicks: Let the children use tweezers to pickup toothpicks and drop them into the holes at the top of a spice jar.

Thumbprint Fun

CHILDREN WILL DEVELOP
Finger Coordination
Eye-Hand Coordination
Visual Motor Control

USE WITH:
Individuals
Small groups

MATERIALS AND SUPPLIES

Stamp pads of various colors
Fine-tipped markers or pencils
Butcher paper

Cut a long sheet of butcher paper. Lay it on the table/floor. Put markers, pencils, and stamp pads around it.

ACTIVITY

Using markers and/or pencils, have the children help you draw small circles all over the paper. Then let the children ink their thumbs on the stamp pads and put all colors of thumbprints in the circles. Hang the **Thumbprint Mural.**

VARIATIONS:

Along The Lines: Draw lines on the paper and have the children put thumbprints on the lines.

Color Creatures: Draw features on the thumbprints to create *"make-believe"* creatures.

Creatures On The Go: Let the children draw cars, trucks, buses, and airplanes with a lot of windows. Have the children put thumbprint creatures in the windows.

Arms In Tubes

CHILDREN WILL DEVELOP	USE WITH:
Finger Coordination	Individuals
Eye-Hand Coordination	Small groups
Upper Body Control	

MATERIALS AND SUPPLIES

Heavy cardboard tubes, large enough for a child's arm to fit through. (Available at carpet stores and newspaper printing offices.)
Small plastic margarine tubs
Buttons
Masking tape

Place several pairs of cardboard tubes on your tables. The tubes in each pair should be between 6" and 10" apart with several feet between each pair. Tape the pairs to the table.

ACTIVITY

Have a child sit at the table and put one arm through each tube. Scatter buttons around the tubes within reach of the child's hands. Put an empty container between the child's hands. Encourage the child to use his thumb and index finger on both hands to pick up the buttons and put them in the container.

VARIATIONS:

More Objects: Use a variety of objects: inch blocks, bingo chips, small plastic bears, etc.

Reach And Sort: Put different objects on the table along with several small containers. As the children pick up the objects, they can sort them into the different containers.

Tongs Pick-Up

MATERIALS AND SUPPLIES

Water table or plastic tubs filled with water   Corks
Ice or cooking tongs   Small blocks
Small buckets with handles   Packing peanuts

Fill the water table or tub about half full of water. Add the corks, blocks, and/or other items that float. Have tongs and buckets available.

ACTIVITY   Let the children use the tongs to grab the floating objects out of the water and then drop them into a small bucket. When all of the objects have been caught, dump them back into the water and play again.

VARIATIONS:

Strainer Scoop: Use different size strainers to scoop up the floating objects and then dump them in the dish pan.

Ice Cube Grab: Float ice cubes made with colored water.

Grab And Sort: Have the children sort the objects they pick out of the water by kind, color, size, etc.

Lie Down: Using tubs of water, have the children lie on their stomachs to do this activity.

Tongs and Balls: Have tongs, ping-pong balls in a bucket, and egg cartons on the table. Let the children pick up the balls with the tongs and place them in the egg carton.

Mixing Colors

CHILDREN WILL DEVELOP
Finger Coordination
Eye-Hand Coordination
Visual Motor Control

USE WITH:
Individuals
Small groups

MATERIALS AND SUPPLIES

Unbreakable eye droppers
Small containers
Ice cube trays

Food coloring
Large bucket

Fill ice cube trays about half full of clear water. Put colored water in small containers. Set the trays, colored water, and eye droppers on a table. Put the bucket on the floor.

ACTIVITY

Using their thumbs and index fingers, have the children draw colored water into the eye droppers and then squeeze it out into any section of the ice cube tray. Continue until each section of water has had color added to it. Talk about the colors as you mix and match them. Dump the colored water into the bucket, rinse out the tray, and add more clear water to play again.

VARIATIONS:

Suncatchers: Drop the colored water onto pieces of heavy white paper toweling or coffee filters. When dry, hang them in a sunny window.

Corn Starch Goop: Pour corn starch onto a large tray or baking pan. Let the children drop colored water on the corn starch. After the children have added enough water, let them explore the mixture with their fingers.

Water Tubes

MATERIALS AND SUPPLIES

Vegetable oil
Colored water
Elbow macaroni
Colored popcorn kernels
Clay

Clear plastic tubing, 3/4" diameter
Small colored beads
Eye droppers
Duct tape

Put the different ingredients in separate containers. Cut the plastic tubing into twelve inch lengths. Plug and seal one end of each tube with clay and duct tape. Put the tubes on the table along with containers of oil, kernels, water, etc.

ACTIVITY

Let the children use eye droppers to fill their tubes with liquids and their fingers to add beads, kernels, etc. Continue filling each tube until it is filled up to two inches from the end. Seal this end as you did the bottom end.

Encourage the children to twist, turn, and shake their tubes while watching the liquids mix and the objects move.

VARIATIONS:

Water Tube Jewelry: Cut longer and shorter tubes and let the children make necklaces and bracelets. Simply bend each filled tube and tape the ends together. Have fun wearing your new jewelry!

Peanut Structures

CHILDREN WILL DEVELOP
Arm, Hand, Finger Coordination
Eye-Hand Coordination
Visual Motor Control

USE WITH:
Individuals
Small groups

MATERIALS AND SUPPLIES

Dish tub
Packing peanuts
Styrofoam meat trays
Round wooden/plastic toothpicks

Fill a dish tub with packing peanuts
and a small container with toothpicks.

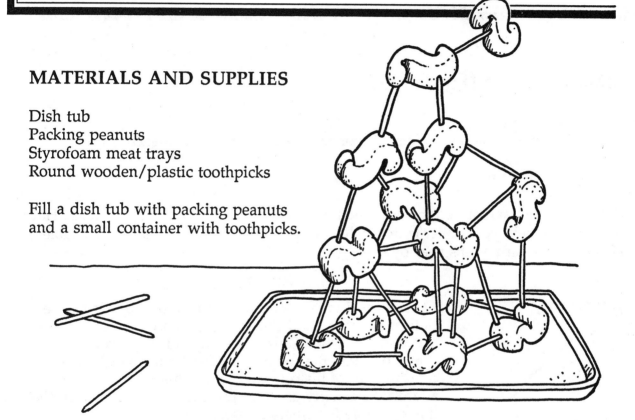

ACTIVITY

Using meat trays for bases, let the children build structures
by connecting the peanuts with toothpicks.

NOTE: Children may want to build their structures in
pairs or small groups.

VARIATIONS:

Individual Structures: If the children are building their
own structures, use meat trays for the base of each one.

Kabob Snacks: Cut cheese into cubes. Wash a bunch of
grapes, take them off their stems, and put them in a large
bowl. Let the children slide grapes and cheese onto
rounded toothpicks. Enjoy the kabobs for snack.

Cotton Ball Pick-Up

CHILDREN WILL DEVELOP
> Arm, Hand, Finger Coordination
> Eye-Hand Coordination
> Visual Motor Control

USE WITH:
> Individuals
> Small groups

MATERIALS AND SUPPLIES

Colored cotton balls
Colored markers, colored stickers, or construction paper to match each cotton ball
Spring-loaded clothespins
Empty margarine tubs

Color code the margarine tubs with the markers, stickers or construction paper. Have the children help you scatter cotton balls on the floor, table, or in your water table. Have the margarine tubs near by.

ACTIVITY

Let each child take a container and clothespin. Using the clothespin, each child should pick up a cotton ball that matches the color on his container and then drop the cotton ball into the container. After he has finished collecting all of his cotton balls, he should dump them out and do the activity again or put the container back so that it is available for others to use.

NOTE: Encourage the children to use only their thumb and first two fingers to open and close the clothespins.
   This activity can be done in a variety of positions on the floor:
   ● Lying on the floor and moving around
   ● Sitting on the floor and scooting
   ● Kneeling on the floor and knee-walking around.

VARIATIONS:

Finger Pick-Up: Let the children pick up the cotton balls with their fingers instead of clothespins.

Scooter Board Pick-Up: Have the children lie/sit on scooter boards as they play.

Alien Clothespins

CHILDREN WILL DEVELOP
  Visual Motor Coordination
  Eye-Hand Coordination
  Finger Coordination

USE WITH:
  Individuals
  Small groups

MATERIALS AND SUPPLIES

Coffee cans   Colored construction paper
Scooter boards   Matching colored clothespins

Cut out spaceships from different colored construction paper and glue one to each coffee can. Draw an alien face on each clothespin. Have the **Aliens**, space ships, and scooters available.

ACTIVITY
In an open area, have the children scatter the **Alien** clothespins on the floor and set the space ships away from them. Have the children ride their scooter boards, pick up the **Aliens**, and return them one at a time to their matching color space ship. Clip each **Alien** to the top rim of the space ship can.

NOTE: Encourage the children to use their thumbs and first two fingers to open the clothespins. Do this activity in a variety of positions, such as lying, sitting, or kneeling on the scooter board.

VARIATIONS:
More Matching: Have the children catch shapes, letters, numbers, etc. and clip them to the space ships.

Paper Tearing

CHILDREN WILL DEVELOP	USE WITH:
Arm, Hand, Finger Coordination	Individuals
Eye-Hand Coordination	Small groups
Visual Motor Control	Large groups

MATERIALS AND SUPPLIES

Styrofoam meat trays (at least one for each child)
Variety of materials to be torn:

Construction paper	Newspaper
Tissue paper	Corrugated paper
Tagboard	Sheets of packing foam
Foil	Waxed paper

Put several different materials to tear in the middle of the table. Have the empty trays nearby for the children to use.

ACTIVITY

Have each child take a tray and set it near him. Let him tear the materials into small pieces and put them on his tray. When each child is finished tearing, he can paste his pieces on paper to make a collage.

NOTE: Encourage the children to use their thumbs and forefingers.

VARIATIONS:

Tear and Sort Class Mural: Have one styrofoam tray for each type of material. Put the trays in the middle of the table. Have the children tear the materials and put each type on a separate tray. After all of the materials have been torn and sorted, make a giant class mural by gluing the pieces to a long sheet of butcher paper.

More Tearing and Pasting: After a child has finished tearing his pieces ask him if he'd like to:
● paste them on a giant block letter, number, or shape
● paste them along a line drawn on paper
● paste them on the outline of a letter, shape, etc.

Grab Bag Wrap-Ups

CHILDREN WILL DEVELOP
- Hand Strength
- Hand Coordination
- Visual Memory

USE WITH:
- Small groups
- Large groups

MATERIALS AND SUPPLIES

Waxed paper
Aluminum foil
Clear plastic wrap
Large grocery bag
3 large trays or shallow boxes

Cut the waxed paper, aluminum foil, and clear plastic wrap into pieces. Put each type on a tray. Have the grocery bag nearby.

ACTIVITY

Have each child choose a piece of waxed paper, aluminum foil, or clear plastic wrap. Then have each of the children find an object in the room and wrap it up in the paper. (If the object is too big, the child can put it back and find another one.) After the objects are wrapped, have the children put the objects in the bag. Let each child have another piece of paper and repeat the activity. do a third time if you like.

Walk around to each child and let her pull one wrapped object out of the bag, carefully unwrap it, and put the object back in the room.

VARIATION:

Grab and Talk: After each child has chosen a package from the bag, have him feel it and then guess what it might be before he opens it.

Sun Catchers

MATERIALS AND SUPPLIES

White glue   Colored tissue paper
Tweezers   Plastic lids from margarine tubs
Meat trays

Let the children tear small pieces of tissue paper and wad them up. Put the wads on meat trays. Set the meat trays, plastic lids, white glue, and tweezers on the table.

ACTIVITY

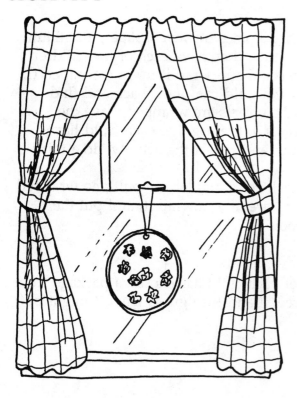

Have the children use their index fingers to spread the glue on the lids. Let them use tweezers to arrange as many tissue balls on the lids as they want. After the **Suncatchers** have dried, punch holes in the them and hang them in a sunny window with a piece of yarn.

VARIATIONS:

Finger Pick-up: Let the children brush the glue onto the plastic lids and use their fingers, instead of tweezers, to pick up the wadded tissue balls.

Bean And Pea Sun Catchers: Older children will enjoy doing this activity with a variety of buttons, dried beans and peas instead of wadded tissue paper.

Sink And Float Snack

CHILDREN WILL DEVELOP
    Eye-Hand Coordination
    Visual Motor Control
    Upper Body Control

USE WITH:
    Individuals
    Small groups

MATERIALS AND SUPPLIES

Bowls   Water
Raisins   Pitcher
Apples   Bed sheet

Fill the pitcher with water. Slice the apples into thin wedges. Put the bowls, pitcher, and food on a tray so that it is easy to carry.

ACTIVITY

Ask the children to help you spread out the bed sheet in an open area. Have everyone wash his hands, get a bowl, and sit around the sheet. Pass the pitcher and let the children pour a little water into their bowls.

After they have poured their water, have each child lie on his stomach by his bowl. Pass the raisins and apples. Let each child take some and put them in his bowl. *"What is happening to the raisins and apples?"* (The raisins sink and the apples float.)

While lying on their stomachs, let the children pick out and eat the raisins and apples.

NOTE: Encourage each child to pick out his snack with his thumb and forefinger.

VARIATIONS:

Sort And Eat: Have a large bowl of the SINK AND FLOAT SNACK. Let the children sort the raisins and apples into two containers and then eat.

Pick-Up Stickers

MATERIALS AND SUPPLIES

Small self-adhesive stickers
Waxed paper

Tape a long sheet of waxed paper on the table.
Lay lots of stickers, sticky side up, on the paper.

ACTIVITY

Let the children pick up stickers with each fingertip on one of their hands. Have them use their other hand to remove the stickers from their fingers and place them, colored side up, on the waxed paper. Let the children switch hands and add more stickers.

NOTE: Encourage the children to keep their fingers separated and spread apart as they pick up each sticker.

VARIATIONS:
Variety Of Positions:
- Kneeling on one knee with waxed paper taped to the wall and the stickers on a nearby low table.

- On their stomachs with the waxed paper taped to the floor and the stickers around it. To make this more manageable, place a long piece of yarn/rope on the floor around the activity.

- Lying on their stomachs with the waxed paper taped to the baseboard of the wall.

The Cherry Tree

CHILDREN WILL DEVELOP
Finger Coordination
Eye-Hand Coordination
Hand Strength

USE WITH:
Individuals
Small groups

MATERIALS AND SUPPLIES

Red clay or playdough
Posterboard or tagboard

Have red clay or make red playdough. Draw a large cherry tree on posterboard and cut it out. Put the tree and the clay/dough on the table or floor.

ACTIVITY

Let the children pinch off small pieces of clay/dough, roll them into balls, and put them on the tree. Continue adding as many *cherries* as the children would like. When the tree is full of *cherries*, let the children press and flatten them with their forefingers.

VARIATIONS:

Squish Again:
Have the children press and flatten the cherries using the tips of different fingers for each cherry.

Stuffies

MATERIALS AND SUPPLIES

Empty 35mm plastic film containers with lids
Pieces of fabric in varying textures

Cut or drill a 3/4" hole in the bottom
of each container. Cut the fabric into
8" squares. Put the containers and fabric
on a tray and set them on a table.

ACTIVITY

Have the children remove the lids from the containers,
tightly stuff the pieces of fabric inside, and then replace
the lids. Let the children pull the fabric out through the
small holes in the bottom of the containers. After the fabric
is out, encourage the children to take off the lids and *stuff
and pull* again.

VARIATIONS:

Stuff Snacks: Have a small cereal box (gelatin or pudding)
for each child. Punch one or two holes in the sides of each
box. Have a large bowl of dry cereal and raisins.
   Have the children wash their hands and then get a
box. Let each child spoon his snack into his box, close
it up, and then eat by reaching through the holes and
pulling out the cereal and raisins.

Stuffing Challenge: Keep the lids on the film containers.
Use the small holes in the bottoms of the containers to
stuff and pull the fabric.

Finger Soccer

CHILDREN WILL DEVELOP
- Finger Coordination
- Eye-Hand Coordination
- Upper Body Control

USE WITH:
Small groups

MATERIALS AND SUPPLIES

Masking tape
Several ping-pong balls

In a non-congested area of your room, put a
12" - 18" *tape line* on the floor. Put the balls in
a container and set it by the tape.

ACTIVITY

Let the children lie on their stomachs on opposite sides of the tape, face each other, and make their *soccer players* with the first two fingers on one hand. Their thumbs hold the last two fingers down to their palms. Put a ping-pong ball on the floor and let the children *kick* it back and forth across the line.

NOTE: Have the children hold up their shoulders, necks, and heads by resting on one of their forearms.

VARIATIONS:

Water Table Soccer: Let younger children *kick* with the side of their hands. Set this up in your water table so that the ball is more controlled.

Lots Of Play: Have a longer *tape line* so that more than one pair of children can play at the same time.

Team Soccer: Play in small teams.

Sticky Fingers

CHILDREN WILL DEVELOP
    Finger Coordination
    Hand Coordination
    Eye-Hand Coordination

USE WITH:
    Individuals

MATERIALS AND SUPPLIES

Bingo chips
Child-sized gloves
Self-adhesive Velcro® dots

Adhere a Velcro® dot to each chip and to the fingertips of each glove. Lay the chips on the table, Velcro® side up. Set the gloves on a tray.

ACTIVITY

Have a child put a glove on one hand. Let him pick up chips by touching the Velcro® on his fingers to that on the chips keeping his fingers apart. After a child has filled his glove with chips he can remove them and put them back on the table. Allow him to repeat, using the same or opposite hand, as often as he would like.

Hand Poses

CHILDREN WILL DEVELOP	**USE WITH:**
Finger Coordination	Small groups
Hand Coordination	
Eye-Hand Coordination	

MATERIALS AND SUPPLIES

Light-colored butcher paper
Colored markers

Cut a large piece of butcher paper and tape it to your table/floor.

ACTIVITY

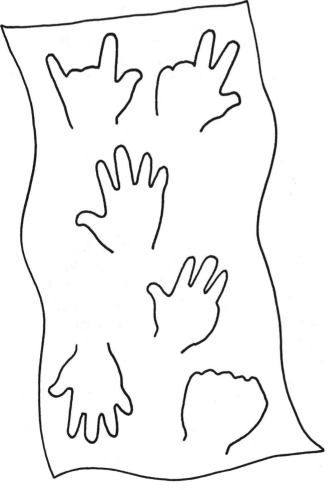

Let each child pose one of her hands on the paper. Have another child or an adult carefully draw around the child's hand and fingers. Ask her if she would like to pose her hand in a different way. If so, trace her hand again. Continue the activity by drawing other children's hand poses. Hang the **Hand Poses** at the children's eye level so that they can have fun matching their own hands to the drawn poses.

NOTE: **Hand Poses** can include one, two, three, four fingers up, a fist, an upside-down hand, a backwards hand, etc. Encourage the children's imagination.

VARIATIONS:

Lots Of Poses: Let the children draw several poses on their own pieces of paper. Encourage the children to trade their poses with friends and try to match their poses.

Sink and Float

CHILDREN WILL DEVELOP
 Eye-Hand Coordination
 Upper Body Control
 Visual Motor Control

USE WITH:
 Individuals
 Small groups

MATERIALS AND SUPPLIES

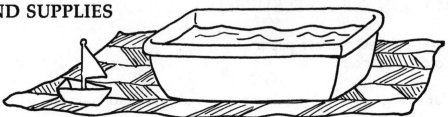

Dish tubs
Objects that sink
Objects that float
Beach towel

Fill the dish tubs about half full of water. Lay the beach towel on the floor and set the dish tubs and container of objects on top.

ACTIVITY

Have each child lie on his stomach in front of a dish tub and put objects in it. Some will sink and some will float. While continuing to lie on his stomach, have him pick out the objects one at a time and put them back. Let him play for as long as he wants.

NOTE: Encourage the children to use only their thumbs and index fingers.

VARIATIONS:
Sink and Float Sort: Make a *"Sink and Float"* chart. When the children take objects out of the dish tub have the children sort the objects on the chart.

Writing Frame Up

MATERIALS AND SUPPLIES

Empty slide frames
Construction paper
Fine-tipped markers and pencils
Removable tape

Set all of the materials on the table. (If you do not have empty slide frames, make your own out of styrofoam trays or posterboard.)

ACTIVITY   Let a child set a slide frame on her paper and draw, color, and/or write inside of it. When she's finished, let her move the frame and draw, color, and/or write some more. Allow her to continue for as long as she would like.

VARIATIONS:

Confined Space: Let the children trace the inside space of a frame all over a large sheet of paper. Encourage them to write letters and numbers, draw shapes and designs, etc. inside each square. Hang it up for everyone to see.

ORAL MOTOR

Color Mixing

CHILDREN WILL DEVELOP
    Control of Facial Muscles, Jaws,
        and Lips
    Breath Control
    Visual Motor Coordination

USE WITH:
    Individuals
    Small groups

MATERIALS AND SUPPLIES

Waxed paper or aluminum foil
Food coloring
4 margarine tubs
Unbreakable eye droppers
Straws
Waste basket

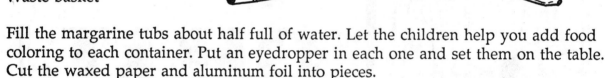

Fill the margarine tubs about half full of water. Let the children help you add food coloring to each container. Put an eyedropper in each one and set them on the table. Cut the waxed paper and aluminum foil into pieces.

ACTIVITY

Let each child put a piece of paper or foil on the table, and then, using the eyedroppers, put drops of colored water on his paper, trying to keep the drops separate. After he has made his drops, let him mix the colors together by blowing at them through a straw. After he is finished mixing colors, remind him to throw his straw away.

VARIATIONS:

In Different Positions: Each time you do this activity set it up so that the children can do it in different positions. For example:
- Lying on their stomachs on the floor,
- Standing at a table, or
- Kneeling on one or both knees next to a low table, bench, or chair.

Oily Mix: Have a container of vegetable oil along with water. Have the children add a little oil and see what happens to their paint as they blow the colors together.

Funny Faces

CHILDREN WILL DEVELOP
Facial Awareness
Eye-Hand Coordination
Control of Facial Muscles, Jaws,
    and Lips

USE WITH:
Individuals
Small groups

MATERIALS AND SUPPLIES

Washable face crayons (For home-made face paint recipe, see Appendix.)
Mirrors
Small containers of water
Tissues
Paint smocks

Before doing this activity send a letter home to your families telling them about it.
Set up a make-up area. Have a small table and chair. Place the make-up on the table.
Put a full-length mirror next to the table and/or a table mirror on the table.

ACTIVITY

Have the children put on a paint smock and sit in the make-up area. Let them dip their crayons into a container of water and color their faces or use the face paint recipe and put it on with their index fingers. Let the children wear the make-up for as long as they want and then wash it off.

Paper Pick-Ups

CHILDREN WILL DEVELOP
Breath Control
Control of Facial Muscles, Jaws
and Lips
Visual Motor Coordination

USE WITH:
Individuals
Small groups

MATERIALS AND SUPPLIES

Plastic straws
Margarine containers
Construction paper or small pictures from catalogs
Meat tray
Waste basket

Cut the construction paper into half inch squares. If necessary cut the straws into shorter lengths. (Some children may not have sufficient breath control to use a whole straw.) Put the pieces of paper and several margarine containers on a large tray or cookie sheet. Have the straws on a meat tray.

ACTIVITY

Let each child take a straw, place one end on a piece of paper, and then, using a long sucking breath, pick up the paper and drop it into a container. Let the children pick up as many as they want and then throw their straws in the waste basket.

VARIATIONS:

Tissue Paper Pick-Up: Use tissue paper squares.

Suck Harder: As the children become proficient, let them use longer straws and/or larger or heavier pieces of paper, such as tagboard.

90

Lovely Lips

CHILDREN WILL DEVELOP
 Control of Facial Muscles, Jaws,
  and Lips
 Eye-Hand Coordination
 Facial Awareness

USE WITH:
 Individuals
 Small groups

MATERIALS AND SUPPLIES

Petroleum jelly
Tissues
Small paper plates, cut in fourths
Mirrors

Set up a make-up area. Have a small
table and chair. Place the petroleum
jelly, paper plates, and tissues on the
table. Put a full-length mirror next to the
table and/or a table mirror on the table.

ACTIVITY   Let the children sit in the make-up area. Put a little
        petroleum jelly on a separate paper plate for each child as
        he wants to play. While looking in a mirror, let the
        children use their index fingers to spread the jelly on their
        lips. After their lips are covered, they can easily wipe it off
        with a tissue.

VARIATIONS:
Edible Lovely Lips: Put peanut butter or spreadable
 cheeses in small containers with scoops. Have the children
 wash their hands, get a small plate, scoop a *spreadable* onto
 it, and then spread it on their lips using their index
 fingers. *"Lick your lips clean. Umm! Good!"* Wipe with a
 tissue and throw it in the waste basket.

Shell Cover-Up

CHILDREN WILL DEVELOP
   Breath Control
   Control of Facial Muscles, Lips,
      and Jaws
   Upper Body Control

USE WITH:
   Individuals
   Small groups

MATERIALS AND SUPPLIES

Washable marker
Large dish pan
Plastic straws
10 small shells

Plastic tray
Dish soap
Beach towel
Waste basket

Put the shells in the dish pan. Cover them with water. Squirt a little detergent in the water. Lay the beach towel on the table and set the dish pan on it. Put the tray next to it. Have the straws and waste basket nearby.

ACTIVITY

Give the children straws and let them blow the water until the shells are covered up by the bubbles. (Add more detergent as necessary.) Now use the straws to blow slow, steady streams of air at the bubbles. Continue to blow until you find a shell. When you do, pull it out and put it on the tray. Continue to blow until all of the shells have been uncovered and are on the tray. Put the shells back in the water, add detergent, and hide the shells in the bubbles again.

VARIATIONS:

More Cover-Up: Use your water table. Collect rocks, shells, stones, sticks, and other things you would find in the ocean. Put them in the water table and play **Cover-Up** with various objects.

Stick Licks

CHILDREN WILL DEVELOP
Tongue Control
Control of Facial Muscles,
Jaws, and Lips

USE WITH:
Individuals
Small groups

MATERIALS AND SUPPLIES

Peanut butter
Tongue depressors
Mirrors
Waste baskets

Put a chair and small table in front of
your full-length mirror. Have the tongue
depressors on a meat tray and the peanut
butter in covered containers. Set the waste
basket next to the table.

ACTIVITY

Sit with a child in front of the mirror. Prepare a *"stick lick"*
by taking a tongue depressor and scooping peanut butter
on the top one-third of it. Encourage the child to lick the
peanut butter off her stick using a *"slow motion"* upward
lick.
 As children are licking, have them look at themselves in
the mirror. *What do they see?* After each child has finished
her peanut butter, have her throw the stick in the waste
basket.

VARIATIONS:
More Licks: Instead of peanut butter, use cream cheese,
cheddar cheese spreads, and so on.

Teddy Bear Hunt

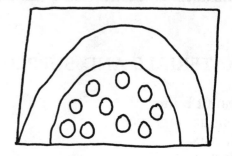

MATERIALS AND SUPPLIES

Large 2" deep aluminum pan
Plastic straws
10 teddy bear counters

Kosher salt
Waste basket

Draw a teddy bear cave on a piece of paper. Draw ten circles inside of it. Place the teddy bear counters in the pan and then fill it with Kosher salt until the bears have been covered. Put the drawing of the cave, the straws, and the pan on the table/floor. Have the waste basket nearby.

ACTIVITY

Give a child a straw and have him sit at the table or lie on the floor with the tray in front of him. Encourage him to blow a slow, steady stream of air through a straw until he finds a bear. When he finds one he takes it out of the pan and places it in the bear cave. Let him or other children continue until all of the bears have been found and the cave is full. Put the bears back on the tray, cover them up, and *"hunt"* again.

VARIATIONS:

More Hunting: Cover popsicle sticks, poker chips, paper clips, flat buttons, or bingo chips with iodized or Kosher salt in deep pans or trays.

Kisses

CHILDREN WILL DEVELOP
    Control of Facial Muscles, Jaws,
       and Lips
    Eye-Hand Coordination

USE WITH:
    Individuals
    Small groups

MATERIALS AND SUPPLIES

Petroleum jelly
Dark construction paper
Small paper cups
Mirrors
Waste basket

Put small amounts of petroleum jelly
in the shallow paper cups. (Individual
portions.) Have a small table with a chair
and mirror. Put the cups of jelly on a nearby
shelf and construction paper on the table.

ACTIVITY
When a child wants to play, have him sit in front of the
mirror. Hand him a cup of jelly. Let him use his index
finder to slowly spread the petroleum jelly on his lips and
then *"kiss"* his construction paper. Reapply more of the
jelly if he'd like and continue to play.

95

Shaving

CHILDREN WILL DEVELOP	USE WITH:
Facial Awareness	Individuals
Eye-Hand Coordination	Small groups
Control of Facial Muscles, Jaws, and Lips	

MATERIALS AND SUPPLIES

Full-length mirror
Shaving cream
Paint smocks/large shirts
Popsicle sticks

Small paper plates
Small bowls of water
Paper towels
Waste basket

Set up a shaving area with a small table and your full-length mirror set upright or on the side. Put the supplies on the table. Have the *"shaving smocks"* available.

ACTIVITY

Have the children put on their shaving smocks and sit/ stand in front of the mirror. Squirt shaving cream on a plate for each child. Let him use his fingers to put the shaving cream on his face. As he is spreading the shaving cream, talk about what parts of his face he is covering.

After *"lathering up"* let him shave with his popsicle stick. Remember to dip the stick into the water between strokes. After shaving let him wipe off his face with a paper towel and throw it in the waste basket.

NOTE: Remind the children not to put the cream near their eyes or in their mouths.

VARIATIONS:

Wipe-Offs: Use a variety of objects to wipe off the shaving cream, such as: cotton balls, small paint brushes, or small sponge squares.

Only Fingers: Let the children use their index fingers to shave off the cream.

Colorful Cream: Color the shaving cream with a little food coloring. Encourage the children to shave with different colors. Talk about how they look.

96

Ghost Faces

CHILDREN WILL DEVELOP
   Facial Awareness
   Eye-Hand Coordination
   Control of Facial Muscles,
      Jaws, and Lips

USE WITH:
   Individuals
   Small groups

MATERIALS AND SUPPLIES

Cornstarch
Clean one-inch, flat paint brushes
Mirrors
Small containers

Set up a make-up area. Have a small table, chairs, and full-length or table mirror. Put small containers of cornstarch, several paint brushes, and cotton balls on the table.

ACTIVITY Have the children sit in front of the mirror and gently brush cornstarch on their foreheads, noses, cheeks, and chins to make **Ghost Faces**. Let them decide whether to brush the cornstarch off of their faces or leave it on.

97

Straws And Balls

CHILDREN WILL DEVELOP
    Breath Control
    Control of Facial Muscles, Jaws,
      and Lips
    Upper Body

USE WITH:
    Small groups

MATERIALS AND SUPPLIES

Wrapping paper   Waxed paper
Tissue paper   Straws
Plastic wrap   Masking tape
Aluminum foil   Waste basket

Cut the straws into various lengths and put them in a container. Cut the paper into 6" squares and set them on meat trays. Put two lengths of masking tape on the floor approximately 10'-15' apart.

ACTIVITY

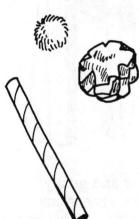

Have each child choose a square of paper, wad it up to make a *"ball,"* and put it on the starting line. Lying on their stomachs, have the children use their straws to blow their balls across the floor to the other line and then back again to the starting line. Let them do it as often as they would like. When finished, remind the children to throw their used straws in the waste basket.

VARIATIONS:

Hit The Target: Cut an 8"x28" piece of posterboard. Color large circles on the bottom edge of the board. Tape the board to the wall at the baseboard. Have the children pick straws and blow ping-pong balls at the target. When finished, have each child throw his straw away.

More Challenging:
- Do it on carpeting.
- Use pom-poms instead of paper wads.
- Increase the length of each straw by taping two straws together.
- Do the activity on scooter boards.

Back And Forth: Have the tape closer together so that the children can lie down and blow the ball back and forth to each other.

Park The Cars

MATERIALS AND SUPPLIES

Small metal or plastic cars
Straws (at least one per child)
Empty cardboard milk cartons with tops cut off
Waste basket

Put the cars in a dish tub. Tape the milk cartons (garages) on their sides on the floor in a random order. Put the tub of cars nearby.

ACTIVITY

When a child wants to play have her choose a straw and set one or more cars on the floor at least one foot from the garages. Let her *"park"* her car/s by blowing them into the milk carton garages. Continue until all of the cars are parked. Remind her to throw her straw away.

99

Cotton Ball Rally

CHILDREN WILL DEVELOP
Breath Control
Control of Facial Muscles, Jaws,
and Lips
Motor Planning

USE WITH:
Small groups
Large groups

MATERIALS AND SUPPLIES

Cotton balls
Straws
Several cups

Waste basket
Tray

Put several cups on a small table or the floor. Have cotton balls and straws on a tray. (If necessary cut the straws into shorter lengths.) Set the tray approximately 10' from the cups.

ACTIVITY

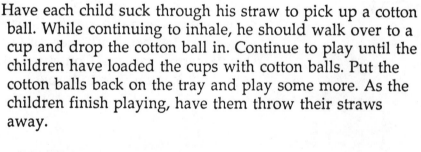

Have each child suck through his straw to pick up a cotton ball. While continuing to inhale, he should walk over to a cup and drop the cotton ball in. Continue to play until the children have loaded the cups with cotton balls. Put the cotton balls back on the tray and play some more. As the children finish playing, have them throw their straws away.

VARIATIONS:

Suck And Drop: Set the tray of cotton balls next to a large container such as a dish tub. Let the children suck up the cotton balls with their straws and drop them into the container.

More Challenging:
● Crawl instead of walk to the tubs.
● Use longer straws thus requiring more breath control.

Teddy Bear Transport

CHILDREN WILL DEVELOP
Control of Facial Muscles, Jaws,
and Lips
Upper Body Control
Motor Planning

USE WITH:
Individuals
Small groups
Large groups

MATERIALS AND SUPPLIES

Teddy bear counters
7 oz disposable cups
Scooter boards
Dish tub
Waste basket
Masking tape

Put two lengths of masking tape on the floor several feet apart. Put the empty dish tub on one line. Put several scooters, the teddy bear counters, and the cups on the other line. Have the waste basket nearby.

ACTIVITY

Have each child lie on her stomach on a scooter board, put a teddy bear in her cup, and hold it with her teeth. Have her scoot over to the dish tub, take the cup out of her teeth, and drop her teddy bear into the tub.

Let the children continue transporting teddy bears until they have all been delivered to the tub. Set the game up again and have more fun. Have the children throw their cups away after they have finished playing.

VARIATIONS:

Special Snack: Use Teddy Bear Grahams® instead of teddy bear counters. Let the children transport their Teddy Bears Grahams® to plates at the snack table, wash their hands and enjoy snack with a drink.

More Challenging:
- Increase the distance between the lines of tape.
- Tape a curved path on the floor to follow.
- Put obstacles on the floor for the children to go around.

Through the Tunnels

CHILDREN WILL DEVELOP
Breath Control
Control of Facial Muscles, Jaws,
    and Lips
Motor Planning

USE WITH:
Individuals
Small groups
Large groups

MATERIALS AND SUPPLIES

Straws
Ping-pong balls or cotton balls
Sheets of paper
Masking tape
Waste basket

Put a 15'-20' curved masking tape
road on the floor. Using the paper,
form tunnels along the road. Tape
them down. Set the straws and balls
at the beginning of the road.

ACTIVITY

Let the children blow the balls along the road and through
the tunnels. Allow them to travel the road as many times
as they would like and then throw their straws in the
waste basket.

NOTE: Cut the full length straws down if blowing through
them seems too difficult for your children.

VARIATIONS:

Two-Lane Highway: Set up two roads which run parallel
to each other.

Speedway: Lengthen the road and make the curves sharper
or wider.

Beachball Blowout

CHILDREN WILL DEVELOP
    Breath Control
    Control of Facial Muscles, Jaws,
        and Lips
    Motor Planning

USE WITH:
    Individuals
    Small groups

MATERIALS AND SUPPLIES

Party favor blowouts
Small beachballs
String
Sturdy stools or chairs

Write each child's name on one of the
blowouts. Hang the beachballs from the
ceiling using varying lengths of string.
(All need to be within the children's reach.)

ACTIVITY

Have the children sit on stools or chairs, about two feet
from the balls. Have them try to touch or move the
beachballs by blowing the party favors at them. How far
away can they sit and still touch the ball? How much does
the beachball move?

VARIATIONS:

Under The Table: Hang beachballs from the sides of a
table and have the children lie on their stomachs while
doing the activity.

Dueling Beachballs: Have two or more children do this
activity at the same time by having them stand/sit on
different sides of the beachball and move it back and forth
with their blowouts.

Party Favor Bubble Pop

CHILDREN WILL DEVELOP
Control of Facial Muscles, Jaws,
and Lips
Breath Control
Motor Planning

USE WITH:
Small groups

MATERIALS AND SUPPLIES

Party favor blowouts
Bubble mixture
Bubble wands

Write each child's name on a blowout.

ACTIVITY

Have the children sit in a circle. Give each one his blowout.
You sit in the middle with the bubble mixture and slowly
blow bubbles towards the children. They try to pop them
by blowing through their blowouts at the bubbles as they
float by. After awhile, have the children change positions
and play some more:
- Kneel on both knees.
- Kneel on one knee.
- Stand.
- Lie on stomachs or backs.
- Sit on large balls or blocks.

VARIATIONS:

Bubble Chase: Blow bubbles outside. Have the children
chase the bubbles and pop them with their hands before
they float away.

More Bubbles: Have several bubble wands and let the
children blow their own bubbles.

Bubble Fun

CHILDREN WILL DEVELOP
- Breath Control
- Control of Facial Muscles, Jaws, and Lips
- Visual Motor Control

USE WITH:
- Individuals
- Small groups
- Large groups

MATERIALS AND SUPPLIES

Beach towel	Bubble solution (water and dish detergent)
Waste basket	Toilet paper tubes
Blowing toys	2 - 4 straws taped together
Bubble wands	Hand with index finger and thumb touching

Using water and liquid dish detergent make the bubble solution with the children in a large wash tub or your water table. Put beach towels under the tub/table to absorb excess water. (Safety!)

ACTIVITY

Let the children stand around the table/tub and make bubbles using the variety of toys and objects.

VARIATIONS:

New Solutions: Add food coloring, scents, and soap to make different bubble solutions.

Bubble Partners: Let the children work in pairs with one child blowing bubbles and the other one popping them with his hands or feet. Switch back and forth.

Down On The Job: Mix the bubble solution in a large tub. Put it on the floor or very low shelf. (Remember the beach towels.) Encourage the children to blow or blow and pop bubbles while lying or sitting around the container. They can:
- Lie on their stomachs
- Lie on a cushion or large ball.
- Sit on a chair, ball, hoppity-hop, or low stool.

Textured Yummy Snacks

CHILDREN WILL DEVELOP
Control of Facial Muscles, Jaws, and Lips
Facial Awareness

USE WITH:
Individuals
Small groups

MATERIALS AND SUPPLIES

Napkins
Plates or bowls
Tableware
Untextured Foods
  Pudding
  Yogurt
  Gelatin
  Applesauce
  Frozen yogurt
  Milk shakes
  Peanut butter
  Fruit spread

Textured Additions
  Low-fat granola
  Crunchy cereals
  Carob chips
  Raisins
  Pieces of apple
  Pieces of carrot

Choose an untextured food and one or more of the textured additions each time you do this activity. Put the main food in a large bowl and the textured food in smaller bowls. Have spoons or scoops.

ACTIVITY

Have the children wash their hands and then help you prepare the snack. Let each child add some of the textured food to the main food and then stir until the texture is completely mixed in.

After the snack has been prepared have the children get their place settings and sit down at the table. Pass the snack and enjoy eating together. Talk about the *"texture"* as you eat.

"Drink It" Snacks

CHILDREN WILL DEVELOP
Control of Facial Muscles, Jaws, and Lips
Breath Control
Upper Body Control

USE WITH:
Individuals
Small groups

MATERIALS AND SUPPLIES

Small pitchers
Small bowls
Disposable cups

Straws
Ingredients to prepare snack

Put the ingredients and utensils to make the snack on a tray. Set the tray on the table.

ACTIVITY

Choose one type of drinkable snack each time you do this activity. Here are some choices to begin with:
- Yogurt
- Pudding
- Applesauce
- Room temperature unsweetened gelatin dessert
- Fruit shakes
- Milk shakes

Wash your hands and then prepare the snack. Pour it into pitchers or spoon it into bowls. Have each child get a cup. Pass the bowls/pitchers around and let each child put his snack into his cup. Give the children straws to drink their snacks.

VISUAL CONTROL

Ping-Pong Pass

CHILDREN WILL DEVELOP
Visual Control
Eye-Hand Coordination
Upper Body Control

USE WITH:
Small groups
Large groups

MATERIALS AND SUPPLIES

Plastic squeeze bottles or turkey basters
Ping-pong balls

Record
Record player

ACTIVITY

Have several children lie on their stomachs in a circle on the floor. Give each child a squeeze bottle and put a ping-pong ball on the floor in front of one of the children.

Start the music. Let the children pass the ball back and forth across the floor or around the circle by squeezing air out of the squeeze bottles. When the music ends the children stop squeezing their bottles, and the child who has the ball holds it still with her hand. When the music begins, the children start passing the ball around again. Keep playing in this manner.

VARIATIONS:

Partner Ping-Pong: Have the children play in pairs passing the ping-pong ball back and forth while lying on the floor facing each other.

Solo Ping-Pong: One child blows the ping-pong ball against the wall, lets it bounce off, and blows it back again.

Be Careful Ping-Pong: Have the children stand around a table and pass the ball attempting to keep it on the table.

Beachball Volleyball

CHILDREN WILL DEVELOP	USE WITH:
Visual Control	Small groups
Eye-Hand Coordination	Large groups
Upper Body Control	

MATERIALS AND SUPPLIES

Small inflated beachball
Clothesline/yarn

Cut a 6' or longer piece of clothesline/yarn. Make the *"volleyball net"* by tying the rope between two chairs approximately 20" off the floor.

ACTIVITY Let the children sit on each side of the net and volley the beachball back and forth by gently tapping it with one or two hands.

VARIATIONS:
Other Positions:
- Have the children sit on their knees and hit the ball with two hands.

- Have the children lie on their stomachs holding up their shoulders, necks and heads by resting on their forearms.

111

Spider Web

CHILDREN WILL DEVELOP
> Visual Control
> Motor Planning
> Position in Space

USE WITH:
> Small groups
> Large groups

MATERIALS AND SUPPLIES

Ball of string or yarn

Make a web by wrapping the string/yarn around, between, over and under chairs, tables and other furniture in a quiet area of the classroom. Be certain that some of the string/yarn is high and some of it is low.

ACTIVITY

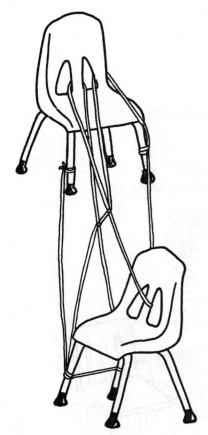

Call on one child at a time to move through the web trying not to touch the string/yarn. Have her find and stand in her own *space* or *house*. After all of the children are in the web, call out one or two of their names. They move to a new *space*. Call on several more children to find new *spaces*. Repeat this several times. Continue calling on *spiders* to move to new homes.

At the end of the activity, have the children freeze in their spaces. Begin rewinding the string/yarn giving the ball of string to the first child that you come to. That child continues rewinding the string/yarn giving it to the next child he comes to. Continue this until all of the string has been rewound and every child has had a chance to rewind a section.

VARIATIONS:

Only Under/Over: Have the children only go under or only over the string.

Permanent Web: Leave the web set up in one section of the room for as long as the children use it.

Catch The Spiders: Using clothespins, hang paper spiders on the web. Have the children collect them by moving over, under, and through the web.

Sink The Ship

CHILDREN WILL DEVELOP
    Visual Control
    Eye-Hand Coordination
    Hand Strength

USE WITH:
    Individuals
    Small groups

MATERIALS AND SUPPLIES

Beach towel
Water table or plastic tub
Squeeze bottles, such as those for ketchup and mustard
Spray bottles which are turned on the *"stream"* setting
Small plastic boats

Fill the squeeze bottles and the water table or plastic tub with water. Lay a large beach towel under the water table/tub. Put the boats in the water.

ACTIVITY

Let the children spray water at the boats trying to tip them over or sink them.

VARIATIONS:

Colored Water Spray: Use colored water in the squeeze bottles.

Lids And Caps: Float jar lids and bottle caps in the water. Fill eye droppers with water and drop water on the lids and caps until they sink.

Water Balloon Writers

CHILDREN WILL DEVELOP
Visual Motor Coordination
Hand Control
Arm, Hand, Finger Coordination

USE WITH:
Small groups
Large groups

MATERIALS AND SUPPLIES

Long plastic *"sleeves"* which newspapers are delivered
Pin
Water
Chalk

Make water balloons with the children. To make each one: Partially fill a plastic sleeve with water. Tie it tight. Cut off the excess plastic.
  Put the *"water balloons"* in a bucket and carry them outside.

ACTIVITY:

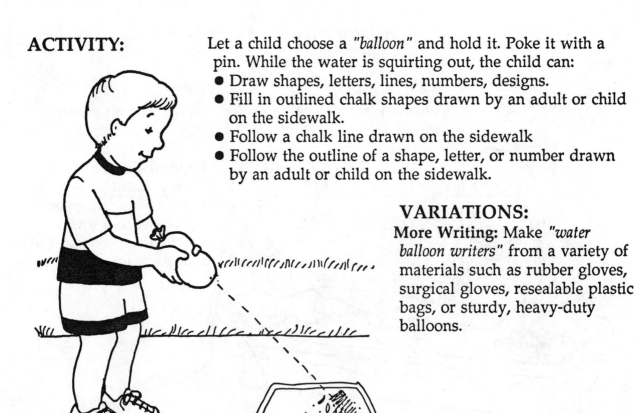

Let a child choose a *"balloon"* and hold it. Poke it with a pin. While the water is squirting out, the child can:
- Draw shapes, letters, lines, numbers, designs.
- Fill in outlined chalk shapes drawn by an adult or child on the sidewalk.
- Follow a chalk line drawn on the sidewalk
- Follow the outline of a shape, letter, or number drawn by an adult or child on the sidewalk.

VARIATIONS:
More Writing: Make *"water balloon writers"* from a variety of materials such as rubber gloves, surgical gloves, resealable plastic bags, or sturdy, heavy-duty balloons.

Around The Stencils

CHILDREN WILL DEVELOP
    Visual Motor Control
    Eye-Hand Coordination
    Visual Control

USE WITH:
    Individuals
    Small groups

MATERIALS AND SUPPLIES

Bingo markers
Large plastic stencils or cut your
  own from styrofoam trays
Butcher paper
Removable tape

Tape a long sheet of butcher paper to your table or floor. Using removable tape, fasten a variety of stencils to the paper. Have a container of Bingo markers nearby.

ACTIVITY

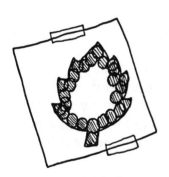

Let the children daub around the inside edge of the stencil. Encourage them to daub carefully, overlapping each dot so that the outline of the stencil is clearly shown on the paper.

After the children have daubed the stencils, have them help you decide which stencils to remove and which ones to keep in place. Remove the tape and take off the stencils they chose. (Save the stencils to use again.) Hang the colorful mural on your wall or door.

VARIATIONS:

Fill The Stencil: Have the children fill the inside of the whole stencil so that a solid picture shows.

Sponge Stencils: Use small pieces of sponge instead of the Bingo markers.

Daub The Outside Edges: Use the stencil insets (the parts cut out of the stencil) and have the children daub around the outside edges of the shapes.

Road Construction - Phase I

CHILDREN WILL DEVELOP
Visual Control
Eye-Hand Coordination
Motor Planning

USE WITH:
Individuals
Small groups

MATERIALS AND SUPPLIES
Small vehicles
Blocks

Put the road construction blocks
in a big box.

ACTIVITY

Have the children sit on the floor in a large clear space. Start building a road by putting 4 - 5 blocks end-to-end. Let the children continue the road construction by taking out blocks from the box and attaching them to the others, making sure that each block is touching the one next to it. *(You don't want any potholes in your road!)*

As the children are constructing the road, encourage them to build in different directions, thus creating a winding, curving road. After the road is completed, bring out the vehicles and let the children drive on their road, following it carefully and slowly. *No accidents, please.*

VARIATIONS:

On The Road: Have small road signs, trees, and buildings which the children can easily put along the road to enhance their creative play.

Road Construction - Phase II

CHILDREN WILL DEVELOP
Visual Control
Eye-Hand Coordination
Motor Planning

USE WITH:
Small groups

MATERIALS AND SUPPLIES
81/2" x11" paper
Colored wide markers
Toy vehicles in a variety of sizes
Removable tape

Have paper and markers handy. Put a dot on the left side of each piece of paper.

ACTIVITY

Let each child construct a portion of the road by drawing a line on a piece of paper which starts at the left side and continues to the other edge.

After the children have built their portions of the *road*, let them place their papers next to each other on the floor so that the lines connect. Tape them together and then tape the entire *road* to the floor. Let the children drive their vehicles on the *road*.

VARIATIONS:

On The Road Again: Have each child draw his part of the road on 3"x5" cards. Construct the road on the table or floor. Drive small vehicles along this road.

Red Cars Run On The Red Road

MATERIALS AND SUPPLIES

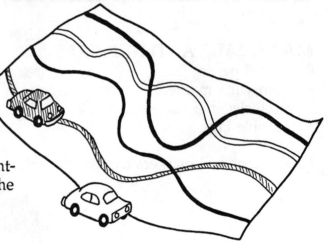

Large piece of butcher paper (3'x6')
Broad-tipped markers (4 colors)
Small vehicles (same colors as markers)

Let the children help you draw 4 different-colored wide roads on the paper. Have the container of vehicles near the paper.

ACTIVITY

Let the children choose vehicles and drive them on the roads that match the colors of their vehicles. Encourage them to trade-in their vehicles and drive on different roads.

VARIATIONS:

Build A Town: Tape trees, bridges, buildings, etc. along several roads.

Where Are You Going? Tape pictures of stores, restaurants, houses, etc. at the beginning and end of each road. Have the children talk about where they are going and where they have been.

Up, Up, And Away: Draw colored runways and let the children fly matching colored airplanes. Warm them up on the runways, take off flying around the room, and then land on the appropriate runway.

Under The Table: Tape the paper on the underside of a table and have the children drive their cars while lying on their backs.

Chip Dot To Dot

CHILDREN WILL DEVELOP
    Visual Motor Control
    Eye-Hand Coordination
    Visual Motor Coordination

USE WITH:
    Individuals
    Small groups

MATERIALS AND SUPPLIES

Bingo chips in a variety of colors
Crayons to match Bingo chips
Butcher paper

Tape a long sheet of butcher paper on the table. Have the crayons and a container of Bingo chips available.

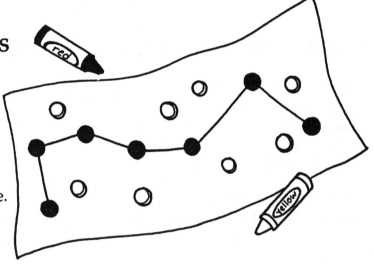

ACTIVITY

Let the children randomly place the chips over the entire piece of paper, spreading them out so that they do not touch each other.

Have the children choose one color crayon, for example - red, and then draw lines from one red chip to another. They can continue drawing red lines until all of the red chips are connected. Have the children choose another color, for example, yellow, and connect all of the yellow chips with yellow lines. Continue this until all of the chips have been connected.

Take the chips off the paper and put them back into the container. Hang the **Chip Dot-To-Dot** for everyone to enjoy looking at and discussing.

VARIATIONS:

All Together: Connect all of the dots no matter what color they are.

By Myself: Children can do this individually by playing the game on 11"x14" pieces of paper.

Fishing For Ice Cubes

CHILDREN WILL DEVELOP
Visual Motor Control
Eye-Hand Coordination
Upper Body Control

USE WITH:
Individuals
Small groups

MATERIALS AND SUPPLIES

Dishpan or water table
Colored ice cubes
Small strainers, ice tongs, spoons in a variety of sizes
Small margarine tubs, small buckets
Beach towel

Fill the dishpan/water table with water and put it on the beach towel. Float the small margarine tubs in the water. Have a bucket of utensils nearby.

ACTIVITY

Float the colored ice cubes in the water. Let the children use the various utensils to fish for the cubes. After each cube is caught, the children should drop it into one of the floating containers or buckets which the children are holding. After the ice cubes have been caught, allow the children to dump them back into the water and fish again.

Shadow Drawing

CHILDREN WILL DEVELOP
Visual Motor Control
Eye-Hand Coordination
Motor Planning

USE WITH:
Small groups

MATERIALS AND SUPPLIES

Sidewalk chalk
A sunny day

Take a container of chalk outside. Set it on the sidewalk or concrete portion of the playground.

ACTIVITY

Play **Shadow Drawing** in partners. To make a *shadow drawing*, one child stands so that his body casts a shadow on the sidewalk. Using a piece of chalk, the partner traces the outline of the child's shadow. The children change places and the first child draws his partner's shadow.

After the shadows have been drawn, the children can play **Shadow Hunt**. To play, the children try to fit their own shadows into the shadow outlines on the sidewalk.

NOTE: Encourage the children to make new and different shadows, such as: bending, stretching, one arm up, two arms out, etc.

VARIATIONS:

Adult-Child Partners: When the children want to take a break from their outside play, have an adult (rather than child) trace each child's shadow.

Paper Shadows: Draw the shadows on paper, instead of concrete, cut them out, and display them in your classroom or hallway.

Magnetic Marble Attraction

CHILDREN WILL DEVELOP
Visual Control
Eye-Hand Coordination
Upper Body Control

USE WITH:
Individuals
Small groups

MATERIALS AND SUPPLIES

Two packages of magnetic marbles
Tape or chalk

Using chalk or tape, make a circle on a rug about 4' in diameter. Let the children help you randomly place one package of marbles inside the circle.

ACTIVITY

Let the children choose different colored *shooter* marbles and lie on their stomachs around the outside of the circle. Have them shoot or roll their marbles trying to hit the ones in the middle. When the marbles hit and stick together, take them out of the circle and put them in a container.

Allow the children to continue to roll the *shooter* marbles attempting to hit as many of the other marbles as they can. After all of the marbles have been hit and removed, put one set back in the middle and play again.

VARIATIONS:

Keep Score: Let each child put the marbles he hits in his container rather than one large one.

Talk About: Help the children count, graph, sort, and compare their marbles.

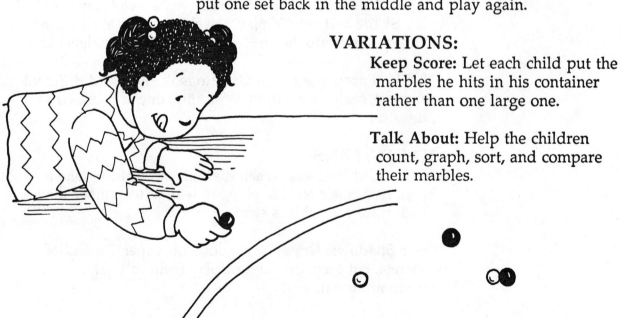

Marble Bowling

CHILDREN WILL DEVELOP
   Visual Control
   Eye-Hand Coordination
   Upper Body Control

USE WITH:
   Individuals
   Small groups

MATERIALS AND SUPPLIES

Six to eight large marbles
Sofa cushion
Three or more empty toilet paper rolls

Put the cushion, container of marbles, and the toilet paper rolls in a quiet, but spacious area of the room.

ACTIVITY

Have the children play in pairs or with an adult. The *bowler* lies on her stomach on a cushion and the other child sits on the floor with her legs spread apart, facing the bowler. The child sitting on the floor stands the tubes on end between her legs. The *bowler* rolls the marbles one at a time trying to knock down the tubes. After the *bowler* has rolled all of the marbles, the children change places and **Marble Bowling** continues.

VARIATIONS:

Keep Score: Let the children keep score as they bowl.

Solo Bowling: One child stands the tubes on end near an empty wall. She lies on a cushion away from the tubes and then tries to knock them down by rolling the marbles at them.

Marble Shoot-Out

MATERIALS AND SUPPLIES

Six - eight large marbles
One bag of smaller marbles
Chalk or masking tape

Make two circles on the rug - one inside the other. The larger outside circle should be approximately 2' - 4' in diameter and the smaller inside circle should be about 12". Put the large target marbles inside the smaller circle. Place the containers of smaller marbles around the outside edge of the larger circle.

ACTIVITY

Have the children lie on their stomachs around the large circle and shoot or roll the small marbles toward the middle trying to knock the large target marbles out of the small circle. Continue playing until the large marbles have been knocked into the large circle. Set up the marbles again and play some more.

VARIATIONS:

On Cushions: Have the children lie on cushions rather than the floor.

Bigger Circle: Draw the outside circle with a larger diameter, keeping the inside circle about 12".

Picture Puzzles

MATERIALS AND SUPPLIES

Light colored construction paper
Crayons
Scissors

Set construction paper, crayons, and scissors on the table.

ACTIVITY

Encourage the children to draw and color pictures large enough to cover or fill most of their paper. As each child finishes his picture, ask him to help you draw several lines and curves from edge to edge thus making a puzzle design. Let the children cut out their pieces. (Help if necessary.) Now the children can put the pieces together to remake their pictures.

VARIATIONS:

Permanent Puzzles: To make the puzzles more sturdy, glue their pictures to tagboard or lightweight cardboard before you cut the art into puzzle pieces.

Puzzle Gifts: Make puzzles for gifts. Put each puzzle in a clear plastic bag and tie it closed with a colored ribbon.

Fingernail Polish

MATERIALS AND SUPPLIES

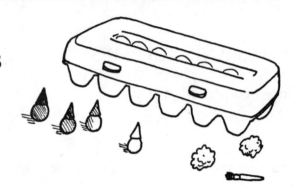

Water
Food coloring
Small eye shadow brushes
Styrofoam egg cartons
Cotton balls

Make different colored nail polish with the children by mixing food coloring and a small amount of water. Put each color in a section of the egg carton. Add the brushes.

ACTIVITY

Let the children polish their fingernails. Maybe they would like to work together, polishing each other's nails. After they have finished polishing their nails, let them decide if they want to let their nails dry or take the polish off. If they want to remove the polish, let them use the cotton balls.

NOTE: Encourage the children to take off the polish one finger at a time.

VARIATIONS:

More Nail Polish: Make the nail polish with petroleum jelly or hand lotion instead of water.

Relax And Polish: Let the children lie on the floor on their stomachs while polishing their nails.

Technicolor Chicken Pox

CHILDREN WILL DEVELOP
Visual Control
Eye-Hand Coordination
Arm, Hand, Finger Coordination

USE WITH:
Individuals
Small groups

MATERIALS AND SUPPLIES

Fine-tipped watercolor markers in different colors

Using the colored markers, put dots, at least two of each color, all around each child's forearm scattering them from the top to the bottom and from the elbow to the wrist.

ACTIVITY

Name a color. Have the children twist and turn their arms searching for that color. As each child finds the color, have her touch the dot with her index finger. As you continue the activity, call out the colors faster - faster - faster --- slower - slower - slower.

VARIATIONS:

Sticker Pox: Use removable stickers instead of markers on the children's arms.

I'll Do It: After the children have done this activity a number of times, have them put the dots or stickers on their own arms.

Colored Cards: Make index cards with matching colored dots and/or the color words written out. Instead of only calling out the color words, hold up the cards as you say the colors or just hold up the cards. This will let the children shift their gaze back and forth from the teacher to their arms.

Punch Outs

CHILDREN WILL DEVELOP
Visual Control
Eye-Hand Coordination
Visual Motor Control

USE WITH:
Individuals
Small groups
Large groups

MATERIALS AND SUPPLIES

Styrofoam plates or meat trays
Sharpened pencils
Soft surface to work on,
  such as a carpet square

Draw a variety of large,
simple shapes on
the plates/trays.

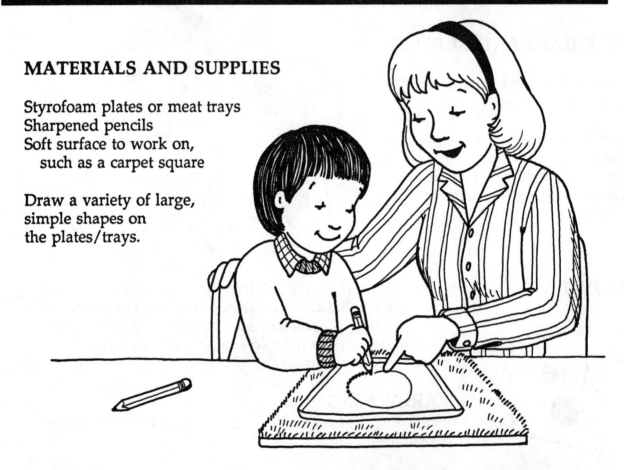

ACTIVITY

Let each child choose the shape he wants and put it on the carpet square on the table. Using a pencil, show him how to punch holes close to each other along the line. After the entire shape has been punched out, carefully remove it from the plate. (The children may want to color their **Punch Outs**.) Hang them from your ceiling for several days and then let the children take them home.

NOTE: Encourage the children to go in one direction. You might sit with a child and point around the line. As you point, he pokes his holes.

Straw Connection

CHILDREN WILL DEVELOP
Visual Control
Eye-Hand Coordination
Visual Motor Control

USE WITH:
Individuals
Small groups

MATERIALS AND SUPPLIES

Markers
Straws
Small containers
Posterboard cut into 12" x 18" pieces

Make **Straw Connection** puzzles. To make each puzzle: Cut a straw/s into various lengths between 1/4" to 5". Lay each piece of straw on the posterboard. Mark the length of each piece on the poster board by drawing a dot at each end. Put the pieces of straw in a small container. Glue the container to a corner of the puzzle.

ACTIVITY

Have the children put their puzzles on the table or floor and then place the straws between the dots that match the length of each straw. Take them off one at a time and put them back in the small container. Play again or try a different **Straw Connection** puzzle.

VARIATIONS:

Make Your Own Straw Connection Puzzles: Older children oftentimes like to make their own puzzles. Give each child a sheet of paper, a marker, and several straw pieces. Have the child place a straw on his paper and draw a dot at each end of it. Remove the straw, choose another one, and draw dots at each end of it. Continue until all of the straw pieces have been used.

Now let the child try and put his own puzzle together. The children may also want to exchange puzzles and complete each other's **Straw Connections**. Put the children's puzzles on the shelf for everyone to use.

Hit The Beachballs

CHILDREN WILL DEVELOP
    Visual Control
    Eye-Hand Coordination
    Position in Space

USE WITH:
    Individuals

MATERIALS AND SUPPLIES

Several different sizes of beachballs
String
Large sturdy ball
Sock balls, yarn balls, or bean bags in a basket

Cut several pieces of string in varying lengths. Tie each piece to a beachball. Hang the beachballs from your ceiling close to a wall. Put a long piece of tape on the floor 2' - 3' from the beachball. Set a basket of balls on the tape.

ACTIVITY

Have a child sit on the large ball and try to hit the beachballs by using:
- Bean bags
- Sock balls
- Yarn balls
- Nerf balls
- His hands.

Dot-To-Dot Body Outline

CHILDREN WILL DEVELOP
Visual Control
Eye-Hand Coordination
Position in Space

USE WITH:
Individuals
Small groups

MATERIALS AND SUPPLIES
Butcher paper
Broad-tipped markers
Crayons

Cut the butcher paper into sheets a little longer than your children's heights.

ACTIVITY

Put a sheet of paper on the floor. Have a child lie on it with his arms and legs away from his body creating a *silly* pose.

Using a marker, outline the child's body with a series of large dots about 2" apart. After you have completed the dotted outline, have the child roll off the paper, get up, and connect all the dots with a crayon. (Encourage the children to go slowly and make their lines as straight as possible.) Now color and add facial features, hair, clothing, jewelry, etc.

NOTE: As you are outlining each child's body, name the body parts you are near. For example, *"I am making dots around your shoulder. Pretty soon I will be going down your arm."*

VARIATIONS:
Dash-To-Dash: Instead of making dots around your children, make dashes which are about 1" apart. The dash-to-dash outlines are much easier to connect.

Memory Dress-Up

CHILDREN WILL DEVELOP
Visual Memory
Eye-Hand Coordination
Body Awareness

USE WITH:
Small groups
Large groups

MATERIALS AND SUPPLIES

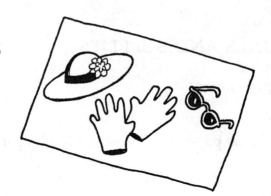

5" x 7" index cards
Dress-up clothes:

Hats	Boxer shorts
Purses	Gloves
Glasses	Scarves
Shoes	Jewelry

Collect the dress-up clothes. Make a set of 10 or more **Memory Dress-Up** cards. To make each card draw three dress-up items on each index card.

ACTIVITY

Spread the dress-up items on the floor so that all of the children can see them. Fan the cards so that they are easy to grab.

Have a child pick a card, study it, and then give it back to you. Have him find the three items and put them on. As the child is looking for the clothes, hold up the card so that the other children can see it. Show the child the card again if he needs help remembering which clothes were pictured. After he is dressed, let the children clap for him. As he is taking off the dress-up clothes, have another child pick a card and begin playing.

VARIATIONS:

More Or Less: Increase or decrease the number of objects pictured on each card depending on the children's skills.

Look And Remember

CHILDREN WILL DEVELOP
 Visual Memory
 Position in Space
 Motor Planning

USE WITH:
 Small groups
 Large groups

MATERIALS AND SUPPLIES
5"x7" index cards

Make a set of 10 or more **Look And Remember** cards. To make, draw three classroom objects on each index card.

ACTIVITY

Fan the cards out so that they are easy to grab. Have a child pick a card, study it, and then give it back to you. Have her walk around the room touching and naming each of the items pictured on her card.

As she is walking around hold up the card so that the other children can see it. Let everyone clap for her after she has touched each object. Show her the card again if she needs help. Play again and again.

VARIATIONS:
More Or Less: Increase or decrease the number of objects pictured on each card depending on the children's skills.

Frame-Up

CHILDREN WILL DEVELOP	USE WITH:
Visual Control	Individuals
Eye-Hand Coordination	Small groups
Visual Motor Control	Large groups

MATERIALS AND SUPPLIES

Butcher paper or plain shelf paper
Ten or more empty slide frames in small containers
Markers

Cut a large piece of butcher paper. Tape it to the table. Let the children watch you trace the inside area of a frame in a variety of positions and angles all over the paper. Put the container of slide frames and colored markers near the paper.

ACTIVITY

Have the children lay the slide frames on the outlines, hold them steady, and color inside the frames. Continue matching and coloring until all the outlines are colored.

NOTE: Leave this set up for at least several days. After the children are finished, hang the **Frame-Up** low on a wall so that the children can easily see it. Keep the container of slide frames nearby, so the children can match the frames to the outlines.

VARIATIONS:

Single Frame-Ups: Make individual **Frame-Ups** on 8 1/2"x11" paper. Let each child use the slide frames to match and color in the outlines.

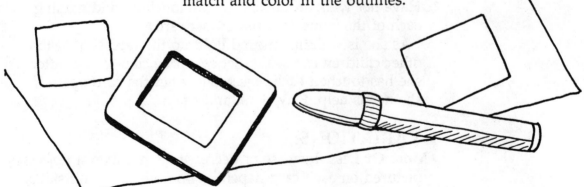

Batting Beachballs

CHILDREN WILL DEVELOP
Visual Control
Eye-Hand Coordination
Arm, Hand, and Finger Coordination
Position in Space

USE WITH:
Individuals

MATERIALS AND SUPPLIES

Small beachball   Paper towel and wrapping paper tubes
String   Clothes hanger rounded out and covered with a nylon

Hang the beachball with a piece of string from your ceiling against a wall so that it falls at the children's height. Put the cardboard tubes and hangers in a large bucket or box and set them near the beachball. (This is also a great outside activity.)

ACTIVITY

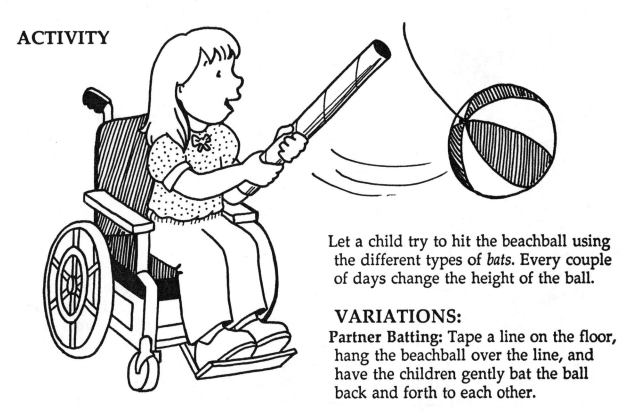

Let a child try to hit the beachball using the different types of *bats*. Every couple of days change the height of the ball.

VARIATIONS:
Partner Batting: Tape a line on the floor, hang the beachball over the line, and have the children gently bat the ball back and forth to each other.

Hand Batting: Let a child bat a beachball using his hands.

Fill The Tower

CHILDREN WILL DEVELOP
Visual Control
Eye-Hand Coordination
Motor Planning

USE WITH:
Small groups

MATERIALS AND SUPPLIES
Cardboard building blocks
Balls of various sizes

Put the balls in a box.

ACTIVITY

Ask the children to help you build a "rounded" tower with the blocks leaving several openings of various sizes, widths, and heights. Make certain there is at least one opening to accommodate the size of each ball.

Have the children take turns choosing a ball, finding an opening that is large enough for it to fit through, and then dropping it through the hole. After all of the balls are inside the tower, take turns removing them by reaching through a hole, choosing a ball that will fit through the hole, and then carefully bringing it out.

VARIATIONS:

More Objects: Use objects from the classroom instead of balls.

Pass And Grab: Build a wall, leaving several openings of various sizes, widths, and heights. Let the children pair up and sit on opposite sides of the wall. One child puts a ball through an opening. Her partner grabs it and puts it down. Then she picks up a different ball and passes it through another hole to her partner. Continue playing by passing balls back and forth through the different spaces.

Flashlight Grab

CHILDREN WILL DEVELOP
Visual Control
Eye-Hand Coordination
Upper Body Control

USE WITH:
Individuals
Small groups

MATERIALS AND SUPPLIES
Flashlight

ACTIVITY

Have the children lie on their stomachs on the floor in a circle. Turn on the flashlight and stand outside the circle. Move the flashlight across and around the inside of the circle. Let the children try to *grab* the light with one hand when it moves near them.

NOTE: When you begin this activity, leave the flashlight on longer and move it very slowly from place to place. As the children gain skill and confidence make the flashes quicker and shorter to increase the challenge.

VARIATIONS:

Flashlight Grab Tag: Play with the children sitting around a table rather than lying on the floor.

137

Grandpa's Beard

CHILDREN WILL DEVELOP
Visual Control
Eye-Hand Coordination
Facial Awareness

USE WITH:
Individuals
Small groups

MATERIALS AND SUPPLIES

Petroleum jelly
Cotton balls
Full length or table mirror
Paper towels
Waste basket

In a quiet area of the room, put your mirror with a table and chairs in front of it. Set the jelly and cotton balls on the table.

ACTIVITY

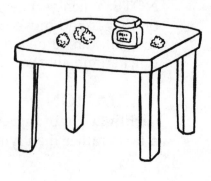

Let the children stand or sit in front of the mirror and use their fingers to put dabs of petroleum jelly on their cheeks and chins. Put a cotton ball on each dab. Continue dabbing and putting on cotton balls until they are finished with their beards.

Let them wear their beards for as long as they would like, then they can take off the cotton, drop it in the waste basket, and wipe off the petroleum jelly.

138

Follow The Light

CHILDREN WILL DEVELOP
Visual Control
Arm, Hand, Finger Coordination
Visual Motor Control

USE WITH:
Individuals
Small groups

MATERIALS AND SUPPLIES

Flashlight

ACTIVITY Have the children sit at a table. Turn the flashlight on. Slowly move the light in a repeating pattern (back and forth, up and down, around in a circle, angle up and down, etc.) on the table in front of one child. That child follows the light pattern on the table with his index finger. Move the light to another child. Change the light pattern and let him follow the new pattern with his finger. Continue playing **Follow The Light**, giving the children different patterns.

VARIATIONS:

Faster-Faster: As the children gain skill and confidence, flash the patterns more quickly to increase the challenge and develop skills.

Follow The Shaving Cream Road

CHILDREN WILL DEVELOP
Visual Control
Eye-Hand Coordination
Arm, Hand, Finger Coordination

USE WITH:
Individuals
Small groups

MATERIALS AND SUPPLIES
Shaving cream
Construction paper (81/2"x11")
Plastic trays

ACTIVITY Have a child take paper or a tray. Let her help you make a straight, curved, or zig-zag road on the tray/paper with the shaving cream. (Repeat with the other children.)
Using her index finger as a car, let her drive on the shaving cream road. As the game continues, trade trays/papers and add shaving cream when necessary.

VARIATIONS:
Textured Roads: Let the children sprinkle birdseed or sand on their shaving cream roads.

More Roads: Use an eye dropper to add food coloring and/or scents to the shaving cream roads.

GROSS MOTOR

Sponge Ball Grab-It

MATERIALS AND SUPPLIES

Scooter boards
Variety of sizes and shapes of sponges and sponge balls
Table
Spring-loaded clothespins
Large box
String

Place a box approximately 12' away from the table. Have several scooter boards nearby. Clip a clothespin to each sponge shape and ball. Slip a piece of string through the hole in each clothespin and tie it closed. Tape all of the strings to the edge of a table.

ACTIVITY

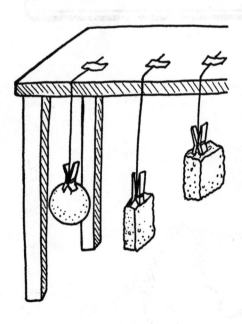

Let the children lie on the scooter boards and pull themselves toward the sponge balls/sponges hanging from the table. Encourage them to grab a ball/sponge and unclip the clothespin using both hands.

While they remain on their scooter boards, have the children place the sponge balls/sponges between their ankles, pull themselves back to the box, and drop the balls/sponges in. Continue playing until all of the sponges are in the box. Clip the balls/sponges back on the clothespins and play again.

VARIATIONS:

Partners: Work in pairs. Have one child scoot over to the table. His partner unclips a sponge ball/sponge and puts it between the first child's ankles. The child scoots to the box, grabs the ball/sponge, and drops it into the box. Switch places and play again.

Dump Truck

CHILDREN WILL DEVELOP
    Body Coordination
    Motor Planning
    Visual Motor Coordination

USE WITH:
    Small groups

MATERIALS AND SUPPLIES

Two large boxes or laundry baskets
Variety of medium to large sized objects:
    Balls, such as beach, playground, sponge
    Empty plastic bottles
    Cardboard blocks
    Plastic bowling pins

Put the objects in one box.

ACTIVITY

Have the children work in pairs; one is the *"loader"* and the other is the *"dump truck."* The *dump truck* lies on her back with her knees bent. Place the empty box at the end of her feet. The *loader* stands behind the *dump truck's* head with the box of objects next to him.

As the *dump truck* raises her feet up over her head, the *loader* places one of the objects between the *dump truck's* feet. The *dump truck* carefully lowers the object and dumps it in the box. After the objects have been loaded and dumped, the children change places and play again.

VARIATIONS:

Sit and Dump: The *"dump truck"* uses his hands to grab an object, does a sit up and dumps the load in the box.

Toe Nail Polish

CHILDREN WILL DEVELOP
Upper Body Control
Visual Control
Eye-Hand Coordination

USE WITH:
Individuals
Small groups

MATERIALS AND SUPPLIES

Water in several small containers
Food coloring
Beach towel
Small eye shadow brushes
Cotton balls

Have the children help you mix colored water in small containers. Put an eye shadow brush in each container. Set the containers on a tray. Spread a beach towel on the floor in a quiet area. Set the tray on the towel.

ACTIVITY

When the children want to polish their toe nails, have them take off their shoes and socks and sit on the beach towel with their legs together and knees up. Let the children spread the *polish* on their toe nails with the brushes. When they are finished, let them decide whether to let the *polish* dry or to wipe it off with cotton balls.

NOTE: Encourage the children to maintain the *"knees up"* position during the entire activity.

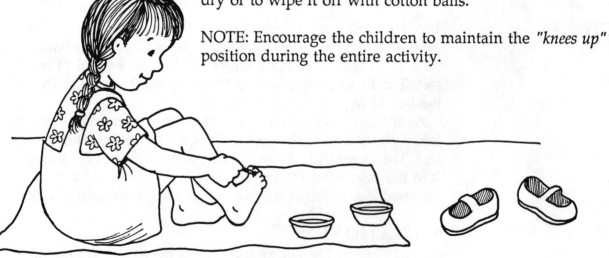

Foot Drawing

CHILDREN WILL DEVELOP
Body Coordination
Motor Planning
Visual Motor Coordination

USE WITH:
Individuals
Small groups

MATERIALS AND SUPPLIES

Butcher paper
Crayons
Carpet squares
Tape

Tape a long piece of butcher paper on a wall close to the floor. Place several carpet squares on the floor in front of the paper. Put the basket of crayons near the carpet squares

ACTIVITY

Have each child take off at least one shoe and sock, choose a crayon, and lie on his back on a carpet square with his feet towards the wall. Have him put the crayon between his first two toes and draw on the paper. After he is finished, have him put his crayon back in the basket and his sock and shoe back on.

Leave the activity set up for several days so that all of the children can *Foot Draw*. When the mural is complete, hang it at the children's eye level for all to see.

NOTE: Encourage the children to lift only their heads and shoulders off of the floor rather than propping themselves up on their elbows.

VARIATIONS:

Sit And Draw: Tape the paper to the floor and let the children sit on stools or large blocks as they draw with their feet.

By Myself: Let the children make individual **Foot Drawings** on large pieces of paper.

Swimming Pool Hide And Seek

CHILDREN WILL DEVELOP
Tactile Discrimination
Body Awareness
Motor Planning

USE WITH:
Individuals

MATERIALS AND SUPPLIES

Small plastic swimming pool or large cardboard box
Styrofoam packing peanuts
Lots of ping-pong balls
2 small buckets

Fill your swimming pool with packing peanuts. Hide the ping-pong balls in the peanuts. Place empty buckets on each side of the pool.

ACTIVITY

Have a child take off his shoes, get into the pool, and use his hands to search for the balls. When he finds a ball have him put it in a bucket. Allow him to keep searching until he has found all of the balls. Hide the balls and play again.

VARIATIONS:

At The Water Table: Fill your water table with packing peanuts and objects. Let the children stand around the table and feel for the objects.

Only The Balls: Hide the balls along with other small objects, such as small blocks and cars, in the packing peanuts. Have the children feel for and find only the balls.

Close Your Eyes: Have the children close their eyes or put on sunglasses and search for the balls.

Under The Table

CHILDREN WILL DEVELOP
Upper Body Control
Eye-Hand Coordination
Visual Motor Control

USE WITH:
Individuals
Small groups

MATERIALS AND SUPPLIES

Sticky dots and stamps
Paper
Bingo markers

Crayons in a basket
Rubber stamps and stamp pads

Tape the paper to the underside of the table.

ACTIVITY

Set up any of these activities for the children to do under a table:
- Lick stamps and put them on the paper.
- Make pictures with Bingo dot markers.
- Draw and color pictures with crayons.
- Make designs with rubber stamps and stamp pads.
- Complete *Dot-To-Dot* pictures.
- Put stamps or Bingo marker dots on the lines which have been drawn on paper.

VARIATIONS:
On The Wall: Set up the activities on a wall instead of under the table.

Puppet Show

CHILDREN WILL DEVELOP
    Body Coordination
    Visual Control
    Visual Motor Coordination

USE WITH:
    Individuals
    Small groups

MATERIALS AND SUPPLIES

Eight or more hand puppets

Set the puppets on the floor in a quiet area of the room.

ACTIVITY

Have the children choose from one to four puppets, take off their shoes, and put the puppets on their hands and/or feet. Have them lie on their backs on the floor and bring their hands and feet together. Let the puppets *talk* to each other.

NOTE: Encourage the children to have their puppets talk, walk, run, jump, dance, and hug their own and the other children's puppets while remaining on their backs and reaching with their arms or legs.

VARIATIONS:

Foot Talk: Two children, while lying head to head, can have the puppets on their feet *"talk"* to each other.

Sponge Ball Pick-Up

CHILDREN WILL DEVELOP
Body Coordination
Visual Motor Control
Motor Planning

USE WITH:
Individuals
Small groups

MATERIALS AND SUPPLIES

Different sized sponge balls or shapes
Big bag or pillow case
Large, low boxes, one for every two children

Put the sponge balls in a big bag/pillow case and set it on the floor next to the large, low boxes.

ACTIVITY

When the children want to play have them take the balls out of the container and put them on the floor next to the empty boxes. Have the children sit with their knees bent and their hands on the floor behind them. Have them pick up the balls one at a time with their feet and drop them into the box.

NOTE: Have the children maintain this flexed position and not lie back on the floor.

VARIATIONS:
More Pick-Up: Use the following items instead of sponge balls:
- Empty milk cartons
- Stuffed animals
- Scarves
- Bean bags
- Empty tissue boxes

Pick the Apples

CHILDREN WILL DEVELOP
Upper Body Control
Visual Control
Motor Planning

USE WITH:
Individuals
Small groups

MATERIALS AND SUPPLIES

Brown, green, red, yellow, and light green posterboard
Masking tape
Several scooter boards

Make 3 large apple trees with the brown and green posterboard. Hang them low on a wall. Make 10 each red, yellow, and light green apples. Tape the apples to a wall opposite the trees.

ACTIVITY

Let each child lie on her stomach on a scooter, pull herself over to the wall, pick an apple, scoot over to the apple tree and put it on the tree. Encourage the children to continue **Picking the Apples** until the trees are full of fruit.

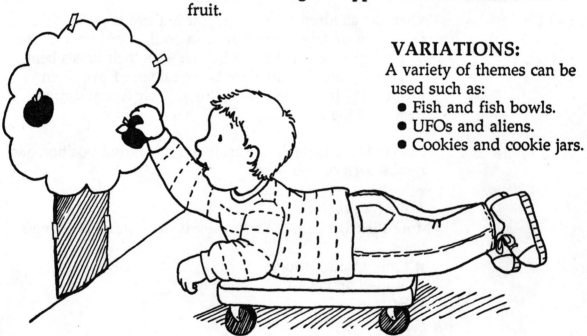

VARIATIONS:
A variety of themes can be used such as:
- Fish and fish bowls.
- UFOs and aliens.
- Cookies and cookie jars.

Button Hunt

CHILDREN WILL DEVELOP
Upper Body Control
Visual Motor Coordination
Motor Planning

USE WITH:
Individuals
Small groups

MATERIALS AND SUPPLIES

Several scooter boards
20-30 paper cups
15-30 buttons in a small cup
Container to be known as the *"Button Box"*

Put the *Button Box*, paper cups, and cup
of buttons on a tray. Put the scooters and
tray on a shelf near an open area. Randomly
place the paper cups upside-down on the floor.
Hide one button under most of the cups.

ACTIVITY

Let the children lie on the scooter boards, pull themselves
around the cups, and check under all of them to find the
buttons. When a child finds a button, he should pick it up,
scoot over to the *Button Box*, and put the button in.
Continue hunting until all of the buttons have been found.
Hide the buttons and play again.

VARIATIONS:

More Hunting: Use other small objects, such as checkers,
inch cubes, teddy bear counters, and Bingo chips.

Crawl and Hunt: Have the children move around the floor
on their stomachs rather than on a scooter.

More Than One: Put 2 or 3 buttons under some of the
cups.

Footpainting

CHILDREN WILL DEVELOP
Upper Body Control
Visual Motor Coordination
Body Coordination

USE WITH:
Individuals
Small groups

MATERIALS AND SUPPLIES

"Paints"
Fingerpaints
Hand lotion
Shaving cream
Liquid hand soap
Ivory Soap® powder and water

Surfaces
Butcher paper
Wallpaper
Fingerpaint paper
Wide shelf paper

Choose the *"paint"* and type of paper each time you do this activity.

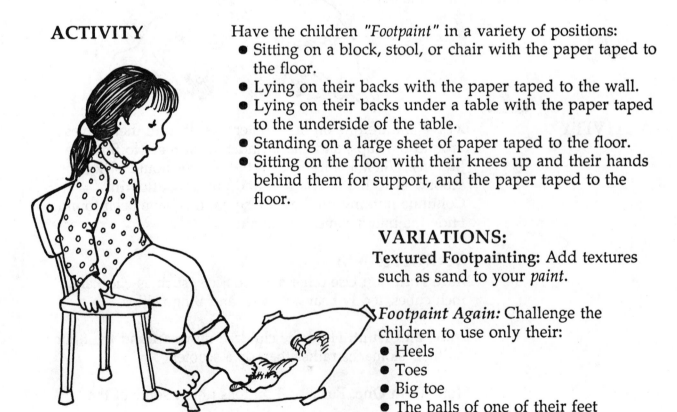

ACTIVITY

Have the children *"Footpaint"* in a variety of positions:
- Sitting on a block, stool, or chair with the paper taped to the floor.
- Lying on their backs with the paper taped to the wall.
- Lying on their backs under a table with the paper taped to the underside of the table.
- Standing on a large sheet of paper taped to the floor.
- Sitting on the floor with their knees up and their hands behind them for support, and the paper taped to the floor.

VARIATIONS:
Textured Footpainting: Add textures such as sand to your *paint*.

Footpaint Again: Challenge the children to use only their:
- Heels
- Toes
- Big toe
- The balls of one of their feet

Stick Ball

CHILDREN WILL DEVELOP
Upper Body Control
Visual Control
Eye-Hand Coordination

USE WITH:
Small groups
Large groups

MATERIALS AND SUPPLIES

Beachballs
Playground balls
Sponge balls
Rhythm or lummi sticks
Paper towel tubes

ACTIVITY

Have the children lie on their stomachs in a circle on the floor. Give each child a stick and have him hold it with one hand on each end. Start the game by rolling the ball to a child. He hits the ball to a friend while keeping both hands on his stick. The children continue hitting the ball to each other, back and forth and around the circle.

NOTE: Encourage the children to keep their legs straight, and their elbows off the floor. Try to hit the ball when both arms are completely extended.

VARIATIONS:
Different Balls: Use a different type of ball each time you play **Stick Ball**.

Grocery Bag Locomotion

CHILDREN WILL DEVELOP
Body Coordination
Motor Planning
Position in Space

USE WITH:
Small groups
Large groups

MATERIALS AND SUPPLIES

Plastic grocery bags with handles

ACTIVITY

Give each child a grocery bag and have him stand in it holding onto the handles.

Play SIMON SAYS. The children can move in their bags as Simon directs.

- Simon says, *"Take one foot out of the bag. Put the foot back in the bag.....Stop."*
- Simon says, *"Walk forward.....Stop."*
- Simon says, *"Walk backward.....Stop."*
- Simon says, *"Jump up and down.....Stop."*
- Simon says, *"Stand still and wave to a friend with one hand......Stop."*
- Simon says, *"Turn around in a circle.....Stop."*

VARIATIONS:

Freeze: Play some music and have the children dance in the bags until the music stops.

Musical Chairs: Use the bags while playing MUSICAL CHAIRS.

Follow the Leader: Lead the children around the room in their bags. Remember to move slowly.

Move: Let the children practice moving in their bags. They can move:
- From one wall to another.
- Between chairs.
- Around obstacles or cones, and so on.

Basters and Buckets

CHILDREN WILL DEVELOP
Upper Body Control
Visual Motor Control
Eye-Hand Coordination

USE WITH:
Individuals
Small groups

MATERIALS AND SUPPLIES

Several turkey basters
Several scooter boards
5-8 plastic containers such as margarine or whipped topping tubs
One plastic dish pan
Towel

Lay the towel on the floor. Place a dish pan partially filled with water in the center of the towel and the smaller empty containers randomly nearby. Have the turkey basters in a coffee can. Put the can near the scooters.

ACTIVITY

Have a child get a baster and lie on her stomach on a scooter board. Have her push herself to the container of water, fill the baster, and push herself to one of the smaller containers to empty the baster. Continue the activity until the dish pan is empty. Fill it and play some more.

VARIATIONS:
A Little Easier: Put the small containers near the dish pan. Allow the children to sit around the tub and fill the small containers with water.

Magic Carpet Ride

CHILDREN WILL DEVELOP
Body Coordination
Motor Planning
Upper Body Control

USE WITH:
Small groups
Large groups

MATERIALS AND SUPPLIES

Magic Carpets such as:
Blankets
Sheets
Throw rugs
Inflated inner tube with rope tied to it

Have the magic carpets in a box.

ACTIVITY

Have the children play with a partner. One child sits on the magic carpet and her partner pulls her around for a ride. After a while they change places and the first child gets a ride and her partner pulls.

VARIATIONS:

Freeze: Play music while the children are doing this activity and have them switch places when the music stops.

Challenge Course: After the children have played several times in open areas, set up an obstacle course using chairs, boxes, and blocks.

Musical Stepping Stones

CHILDREN WILL DEVELOP
Visual Motor Coordination
Motor Planning
Position in Space

USE WITH:
Small groups
Large groups

MATERIALS AND SUPPLIES

Use one or a variety of the following
for *stepping stones*:
Carpet squares
Large wooden or cardboard blocks
Small cushions or pillows
Inner tubes
Low, small cardboard boxes
Foam shapes
Shoe boxes
Record player or other source of music

Make a path by spreading the *stepping
stones* on the floor. Put the *stones* close
enough so that the children can easily
step from one *stone* to the other. Have
the music near the path.

ACTIVITY

While the music is playing, have the children step on the
stones with only one child on a stone at a time. When the
music stops, everyone should *"freeze"* on his *stone*. Start
the music and continue playing.

After playing several times, make the activity more
challenging. Each time the music stops, direct the children
to kneel, sit down, stand on one foot, etc. on their *stones*.
When the music begins again, they continue walking.

VARIATIONS:

Stepping Stone Maze: Use the *"stones"* to set up a maze
around the room for the children to follow as often as they
would like. Change the direction of the maze each time
you set it up.

Stepping Stone Relay

CHILDREN WILL DEVELOP
> Visual Motor Coordination
> Motor Planning
> Position in Space

USE WITH:
> Small groups
> Large groups

MATERIALS AND SUPPLIES

Use one or a variety of the following:
> Carpet squares
> Large wooden or cardboard blocks
> Small cushions or pillows
> Inner tubes
> Low, small cardboard boxes
> Foam shapes
> Shoe boxes

Variety of balls - at least one for each child
Four boxes

Set up the relay. Using the *stepping stone* materials above, make two courses about 20' long. Put the *stones* close enough together so that the children can easily step from one to the other. Put an empty box at the beginning of each course and a box filled with the balls at the end of each course.

ACTIVITY

Divide the children into two groups. Have the first child in each team walk on the stepping stones, take a ball out of the box, carry it to the empty box, and drop it in. The next child does the same thing and this continues until each child has had at least one turn. Clap for each child as he drops his ball into the box.

VARIATIONS:
More Relays: Have the children carry balls in a variety of ways: under their chins, under an arm, above their heads, on a shoulder, etc.

Turtle Race

CHILDREN WILL DEVELOP
> Visual Motor Coordination
> Motor Planning
> Body Control

USE WITH:
> Small groups
> Large groups

MATERIALS AND SUPPLIES

Bean bag chairs or pillows
Masking tape

Put two tape lines on the floor to mark the starting and ending points of the race.

ACTIVITY

Divide the children into two or more teams. Have half of each team stand behind one line and the other half behind the other line. Have the first child on each team lie flat on the floor. Put one bean bag chair/pillow on each child's back.

When you say "*Go*," the children should crawl flat on the floor to the opposite boundary line, careful to keep their turtle shells on their backs. The next child in each line then lies down, gets the turtle shell on her back and continues the race. Clap for each child as she goes over the boundary line. Keep playing until everyone has had several turns.

It's Under the Blanket

CHILDREN WILL DEVELOP
Visual Motor Coordination
Motor Planning
Body Awareness

USE WITH:
Small groups
Large groups

MATERIALS AND SUPPLIES

Large thin blanket or sheet
Small objects which the children will easily recognize by feeling

Button	Marker	Doll
Teddy bear counter	Giant paper clip	Cotton ball
Crayon	Truck	Spoon
Block	Mitten	Book
Eraser	Ball	Shovel
Pencil		

Put all of the objects in a bag or other closed container.

ACTIVITY

Have the container of objects nearby. Ask the children to help you spread the blanket on the floor. Have everyone sit cross legged around it and hold onto the edges with both hands. Keeping it stretched close to the floor, have the children close their eyes while you place an object under the blanket. Then tell them to open their eyes.

Ask a child to find the object by crawling flat on his stomach under the blanket. When he finds it, he should bring it out and show everyone. Everyone call out the name of the object. Put a different object under the blanket and ask another child to go under the blanket and hunt for it.

NOTE: Raise the sheet up just little if a child seems to be having difficulty or is afraid. Remember, each child can choose whether or not he wants to crawl under the blanket.

VARIATIONS:

Use a Flashlight: Let the children use a flashlight as they crawl under the blanket.

Musical Seats

CHILDREN WILL DEVELOP
    Body Coordination
    Motor Planning
    Position in Space

USE WITH:
    Small groups
    Large groups

MATERIALS AND SUPPLIES

Record player or other source of music
Variety of things to sit on:
    Stools
    Hoppity Hops
    Pillows
    Buckets turned upside down
    Balls
    Boxes
    Cushions
    Crates
Different types of chairs:
    High
    Low
    Rocking

Arrange the *"seats"* in a circle with at least one seat for each player.

ACTIVITY

While the music is playing, have the children walk around the circle. When the music stops everyone should sit on the closest seat. Ask several children what they are sitting on. Start the music and have the children get up and walk again. Continue playing **Musical** Seats until the children have experienced sitting on most of the seats.

NOTE: Remember that one of the purposes of **Musical Seats** is to sit on a variety of seats. Do not eliminate any seats during the game.

VARIATIONS:
More Movement: Have the children move around the circle in a variety of ways, such as: crawling, hopping, sliding, jumping, etc.

Body Posing Match-Up

CHILDREN WILL DEVELOP	USE WITH:
Body Coordination	Individuals
Motor Planning	Small groups
Position in Space	

MATERIALS AND SUPPLIES

Butcher paper

Cut the paper into pieces long enough for each child to lie on.

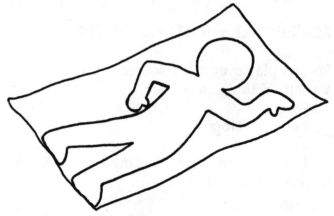

ACTIVITY

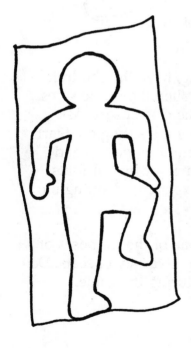

Play **Body Poses.** Have the children practice different body poses. As children wiggle into different positions talk about them. For example, *"Alvin has one arm above his head and the other one at his side." "Carin has both arms out to the side, pointing with one finger on each hand." "Look, Eldo curled up his legs."*

After playing **Body Poses,** let each child pick her favorite pose. Place a piece of paper on the floor and have her lie on it and assume a pose, with her feet at the very bottom of the paper. Trace around her body as she holds the pose. After you have outlined several children, hang the poses on your wall so that the bottom edge (child's feet) touches the floor.

Now play **Body Poses Match-Up.** Let the children choose outlines, stand facing them and try to imitate the poses. Rotate the outlines so that all of your children's poses will be displayed for several days. Each child can take his pose home and play the game with his family.

NOTE: Use dark, bold markers to draw the outlines.

VARIATIONS:

Colorful Poses: Draw the outlines on different colored paper, cut them out, and tape them to the wall.

Hop and Pick-Up

CHILDREN WILL DEVELOP
- Visual Motor Control
- Motor Planning
- Position in Space

USE WITH:
- Small groups

MATERIALS AND SUPPLIES

Several hoppity-hops - one per child
Bean bags
One large bucket or box

Place the box in the middle of a large area (outside, gym, open space in the classroom) and scatter the bean bags on the floor.

ACTIVITY

Have the children sit on hoppity-hops and hop to a bean bag, pick it up, hop to the large box and drop it in. Continue playing until all of the bean bags have been picked up and dropped into the box. Let the children help you scatter the bean bags and play again.

VARIATIONS:

More Pick-Up: Substitute other objects to be picked up, such as paper cups, small blocks, and balls.

Ride and Pick It Up: Let the children ride tricycles instead of hopping on hoppity-hops.

Hop-Hop: Do not use any vehicles. Let the children pretend they are rabbits as they hop to pick up the bean bags.

Roll and Tumble

CHILDREN WILL DEVELOP	USE WITH:
Body Coordination Motor Planning Position in Space	Individuals Small groups

MATERIALS AND SUPPLIES

Wide tape
Large sheet or blanket
Various sizes and shapes of:
    Pillows
    Cushions
    Sponges
    Inner tubes

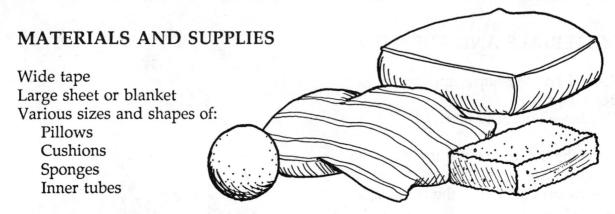

Have the children help you spread the objects on the floor. Cover them with a blanket or sheet. Tape the edges of the blanket/sheet to the floor.

ACTIVITY

Have the children remove their shoes and move across the blanket by rolling, walking, crawling, somersaulting, hopping, etc..

Twist, Turn, Touch

CHILDREN WILL DEVELOP	USE WITH:
Body Coordination	Individuals
Motor Planning	Small groups
Eye-Hand Coordination	

MATERIALS AND SUPPLIES

Magnetic Bingo chips in a container
Magnetic Bingo wands
Cups

Have the wands, chips, and cups on a tray.

ACTIVITY

Let each child choose a magnetic Bingo wand and cup and sit cross-legged on the floor. Randomly spread Bingo chips around the children. (Keep the chips within their reach.) Encourage each child to pick up one Bingo chip at a time with his wand and put it in his cup before reaching for another one.

NOTE: Encourage the children to twist at their waist rather than turning their whole body. Some children might want to explore the chips they collected. Talk about color, count the chips, line them up, sort them, etc. Take your clues from the children.

VARIATIONS:

Twist, Turn, Pick-Up: Use small objects such as inch cubes, teddy bear counters, cotton balls, etc. for the children to pick up with their hands and put in a cup or bowl.

On the Tables: Cut out sets of construction paper feet and tape them to the floor on one side of the table. Place a piece of tape down the middle of the table. Spread the objects on the far side of the table opposite the feet. While playing, the children stand on the feet, bend at their waists, and reach for the objects across the table without moving their feet.

Twist and Sort

CHILDREN WILL DEVELOP
Visual Motor Coordination
Motor Planning
Eye-Hand Coordination

USE WITH:
Individuals
Small groups

MATERIALS AND SUPPLIES

3'x41/2' sheets of butcher paper or tag board
Colored inch cubes or Teddy Bear counters (six colors)
6 matching colored markers
Small bucket

Make several giant **Twist and Sort** game boards. To make each one:
● Draw a large oval in the middle of the board for a child to sit in.
● Draw lots of 6" circles, several of each color, to the left and right of the oval
as well as slightly behind it, thus encouraging the child to twist and turn at the
waist.

ACTIVITY

Put the game board on the floor and have a child sit cross-legged in the middle of the oval. Give the child a bucket of blocks or Teddy Bear counters and have him put them one at a time in a circle that matches its color.

VARIATIONS:

Twist and Place: Make your game boards with the circles all the same color. The children can place the objects in the circles without thinking about colors.

Twist and Sort Together: Double the length of your game board and draw room for several children to sit and play at the same time.

Waxed Paper Skates

CHILDREN WILL DEVELOP
Body Coordination
Motor Planning
Position in Space

USE WITH:
Individuals
Small groups
Large groups

MATERIALS AND SUPPLIES

Waxed paper or paper plates.

Cut at least 8"x12" pieces of the waxed paper for each child or have two paper plates for each one.

ACTIVITY

Give each child two pieces of waxed paper or paper plates. Set them on the floor and put one foot on each piece/plate.

Let the children *"skate"* around the room keeping their feet on the paper and sliding across the floor. They will soon discover that if they lift their feet, their skates will come off.

VARIATIONS:

Around and About: Set up an obstacle course to skate around.

On the Trail: Using masking tape, make trails for the children to skate on.

Stocking Skate: Have the children take off their shoes and skate in their stocking feet.

Circles and Stamps

MATERIALS AND SUPPLIES

3'x41/2' sheets of butcher paper
Variety of rubber stamps
Stamp pads

Make giant **Stamping** game boards. To make each one:
● Draw a large oval in the middle of each piece of paper for a child to sit on.
● Draw 25 to 30, 2" circles on the paper all around each oval. Be sure the circles are spread out, but within the children's reach. (Make enough so that all of your children have lots of opportunities to play this game.)

ACTIVITY

Put a game board on the floor with the stamps and stamp pads within reach. Have a child sit cross-legged in the middle of the oval. Let her choose a stamp pad and a stamp. Have her hold one in each hand and let her ink her stamp and then stamp one of the circles. Allow her to continue inking and stamping until she's finished playing. After the children have stamped all of the circles on a gameboard, hang it on a wall or bulletin board for everyone to see. Repeat often.

VARIATIONS:

Lick and Stick: Have the children lick and stick stamps, putting one in each circle.

Fill the Circles: Fill a bucket with small objects such as inch cubes, Teddy Bear counters, cotton balls, etc. Let the children put the objects in the circles.

Tong Twister

MATERIALS AND SUPPLIES

Several ice tongs
Small buckets or containers

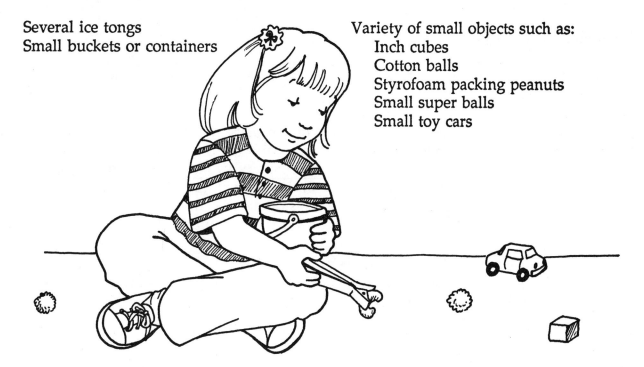

Variety of small objects such as:
Inch cubes
Cotton balls
Styrofoam packing peanuts
Small super balls
Small toy cars

ACTIVITY

Have the children sit cross-legged on the floor. Randomly spread the objects around the children keeping the objects within their reach.

Give each child a pair of tongs to hold in one hand and a bucket to hold in the other. Encourage them to pick up the objects one at a time and put each one in the bucket. When finished, dump them and play again.

NOTE: Challenge the children to remain seated, twisting and turning at their waists to reach the objects.

Tube Massage

CHILDREN WILL DEVELOP
   Body Awareness
   Tactile Discrimination
   Eye-Hand Coordination

USE WITH:
   Small groups

MATERIALS AND SUPPLIES

Beach towel
Small and large cardboard tubes

Lay the beach towel on the floor. Set a bucket of paper tubes next to the towel.

ACTIVITY   Have the children work in pairs with one child lying on the towel getting a massage and the other one giving the massage using a cardboard tube. Have the child with the tube gently roll it on the other child's back, arms, shoulders, and/or legs. Have the children change positions so that the second child gets a **Tube Massage.**

VARIATIONS:
Massage To Music: Play soothing, quiet music while doing this activity.

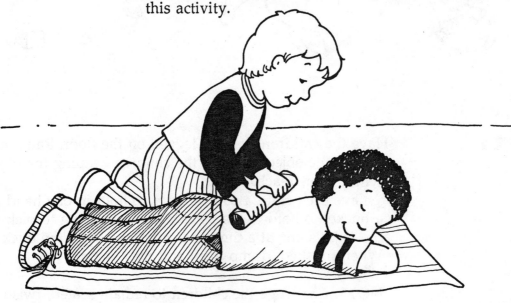

Making Rainbows

CHILDREN WILL DEVELOP

Visual Motor Coordination
Visual Motor Control
Eye-Hand Coordination

USE WITH:

Individuals
Small groups

MATERIALS AND SUPPLIES

Butcher paper
Crayons or markers
Tape
Tempera paint

Cut the butcher paper into a 3-5 foot length. Put it on the floor and tape the corners down. Have several baskets of crayons/markers near the paper.

ACTIVITY

When the children want to make rainbows have them sit cross-legged on the paper near the bottom edge. Mark an X on each side of the child near the edge of the paper; thus the children will be sitting on the paper with the X's slightly behind them.

Let the children use crayons and/or markers to make rainbows by starting at one X, drawing half circles around the front of their bodies, and stopping at the other X. Allow the children to continue drawing the rainbow, making as many lines as they would like. After the children have finished their lines, let them paint between them.

NOTE: While the children are making their arches, encourage them to keep one hand in their laps while drawing with the other. By doing this children will not lean on their unused hands.

VARIATIONS:

More Realistic: Older children sometimes want to be more realistic. Set out crayons which represent real rainbows. Talk about the order of the colors. Encourage the children to do the activity drawing and coloring *"real rainbows."*

Human Bridges and Tunnels

CHILDREN WILL DEVELOP
Visual Motor Control
Motor Planning
Position in Space

USE WITH:
Large groups

MATERIALS AND SUPPLIES

None

ACTIVITY

Divide the children so that some are *"bridges"* and *"tunnels"* and some are *"vehicles."*

Have the *bridges* and the *tunnels* make their positions with their bodies. When you say, *"Start your motors,"* the *vehicles* should start up and crawl over, under, around and/or through the *bridges* and step over *tunnels* trying not to touch them. Allow the children to drive for awhile. Then say, *"Stop your motors."* The *vehicles* should stop and turn off their engines. Have the children change positions, get ready, and start their motors again.

NOTE: Encourage the children to work together to make long tunnels.

Shadow Posing

CHILDREN WILL DEVELOP
Visual Motor Control
Motor Planning
Position in Space

USE WITH:
Small groups
Large groups

MATERIALS AND SUPPLIES

None

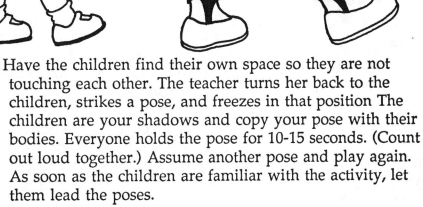

ACTIVITY   Have the children find their own space so they are not touching each other. The teacher turns her back to the children, strikes a pose, and freezes in that position The children are your shadows and copy your pose with their bodies. Everyone holds the pose for 10-15 seconds. (Count out loud together.) Assume another pose and play again. As soon as the children are familiar with the activity, let them lead the poses.

Pose and Hold

CHILDREN WILL DEVELOP
    Body Coordination
    Motor Planning
    Visual Motor Control

USE WITH:
    Small groups
    Large groups

MATERIALS AND SUPPLIES

Whistle or Drum

ACTIVITY

Explore with the children what a pose is and the possibilities of different poses using their entire bodies.

For example:
- On their hands and knees.
- With one arm up and one leg back.
- On their backs with both legs and arms up.
- Hands and feet on the floor with their bottoms in the air to form bridges.

Have each child find his own space in an open area. Tell the children that when they hear you blow the whistle or beat the drum, they should pose and hold it until they hear the whistle/drum again (approximately 5-20 seconds depending on your children). Relax. Let several children hold their poses for everyone to see. Clap for everyone. Play again and again.

NOTE: If the children are limiting their poses, give them specific ideas for poses. For example:
- *"We are going to kneel down for our next pose."*
- *"We are going to do our next pose with at least one arm up in the air."*

Follow the Foot Path

MATERIALS AND SUPPLIES

Plain shelf paper or butcher paper
Red and blue crayons
Red and blue stickers
Tape

Cut 3–5' lengths of shelf/butcher paper so there is one for each child.

ACTIVITY

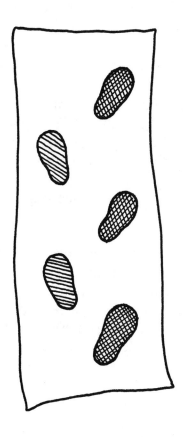

Tape one child's paper to the floor. While he stands at one edge, trace around his feet, using red for one foot and blue for the other. Have him slowly walk across the paper either in a straight forward fashion or changing the position of his feet with each step (right over left, side step, toes pointed out or in, etc.). Trace around each new foot position one step at a time. Remember to use red for one foot and blue for the other.

Continue the foot path with other children by taping each child's paper to the end of the completed one. Keep the **Foot Path** going around the room. The children can color in their footprints if they would like. When the **Foot Path** is finished encourage the children to follow it.

NOTE: To help them you could put red and blue stickers on the appropriate feet of each child who walks the path. This will help the children match their own feet to the drawn feet.

VARIATIONS:

Long, Narrow Highway: For younger children cut out footprints and tape them on a long sheet of shelf paper, varying the length of the *"steps"* depending on your children's skill. Tape the long path to the floor and let the children follow the **Highway**.

Right Over Left

MATERIALS AND SUPPLIES

2' to 4' sheets of plain shelf paper, at least one per child
Red and blue crayons
Red and blue stickers
Tape

ACTIVITY

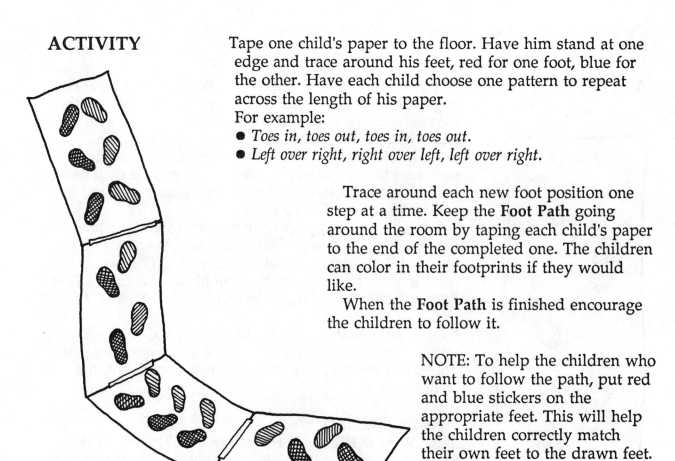

Tape one child's paper to the floor. Have him stand at one edge and trace around his feet, red for one foot, blue for the other. Have each child choose one pattern to repeat across the length of his paper.
For example:
- *Toes in, toes out, toes in, toes out.*
- *Left over right, right over left, left over right.*

Trace around each new foot position one step at a time. Keep the **Foot Path** going around the room by taping each child's paper to the end of the completed one. The children can color in their footprints if they would like.

When the **Foot Path** is finished encourage the children to follow it.

NOTE: To help the children who want to follow the path, put red and blue stickers on the appropriate feet. This will help the children correctly match their own feet to the drawn feet.

178

Rug Roll-Up

CHILDREN WILL DEVELOP
   Body Awareness
   Motor Planning
   Tactile Discrimination

USE WITH:
   Small groups

MATERIALS AND SUPPLIES

3'x5' (or longer) throw rugs

ACTIVITY

Play **Rug Roll-Up** in partners. Put a rug on the floor and have one child lie at one end of it, making sure that her head is not on the rug and her arms are at her sides. Her partner securely rolls her in the rug. When she is all rolled up she rolls in the opposite direction to unroll herself. Encourage the partners to change places so that the children get several opportunities to be rolled and unrolled.

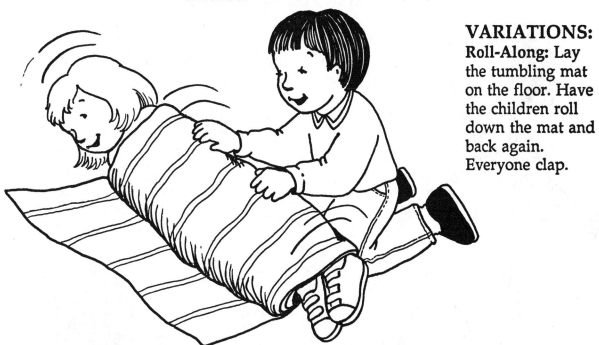

VARIATIONS:
Roll-Along: Lay the tumbling mat on the floor. Have the children roll down the mat and back again. Everyone clap.

Tubing

CHILDREN WILL DEVELOP
Body Coordination
Motor Planning
Position in Space

USE WITH:
Small groups
Large groups

MATERIALS AND SUPPLIES

Several inflated inner tubes
Rope

Tie a three foot rope through the hole of each inner tube.

ACTIVITY

Play **Tubing** with a partner. One child kneels on his hands and knees, sits, or lays on the inner tube. His partner holds the rope and walks around a large open space, pulling the child in the inner tube. After a time, have the children stop pulling, change places, and continue **Tubing**.

VARIATIONS:

Tube to Music: Play music while you **Tube**. When the music stops the partners change places.

Tubing Path: Tape a line on the floor for the child pulling the inner tube to follow.

Tubing Maze: Put chairs, cones, and giant blocks on the floor as obstacles for the children to go around.

180

Queen/King of the Mountain

CHILDREN WILL DEVELOP
    Body Coordination
    Motor Planning
    Position in Space

USE WITH:
    Small groups

MATERIALS AND SUPPLIES

Large blanket or sheet
Variety of materials to build a mountain:
    Pillows
    Large pieces of foam
    Sofa cushions
    Blankets
    Tumbling mats
    Wedge cushions

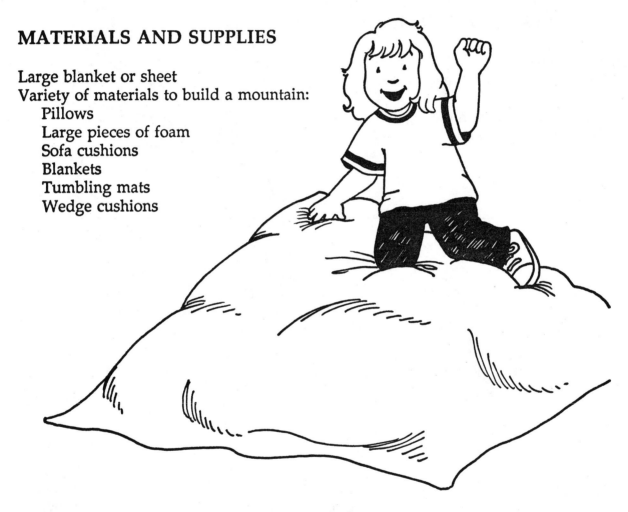

ACTIVITY

Ask the children to help you build a mountain using the various materials. Cover it with the blanket/sheet. Let the children climb to the top of the mountain by crawling, rolling, or walking and then rolling down the other side. (Put a rug or mat on the floor if necessary.)

NOTE: Allow only one child at a time to climb the mountain.

Block Buster

CHILDREN WILL DEVELOP
Visual Motor Control
Motor Planning
Position in Space

USE WITH:
Small groups
Large groups

MATERIALS AND SUPPLIES

Large tumbling mat
4-6 large cardboard building blocks.

Put the tumbling mat on the floor.
Set the blocks at one end.

ACTIVITY

Build a tower with the children at one end of the mat. Let a child roll across the mat, into the blocks, knocking them down. Everyone claps. The child who knocked down the blocks rebuilds the tower before the next child begins to roll. Play **Block Buster** over and over again.

VARIATIONS:
More Block Busters: Have the children crawl, duck-walk, crab-walk, etc. across the mat and knock down the blocks.

Scooter Board Tug

CHILDREN WILL DEVELOP
Body Coordination
Eye-Hand Coordination
Upper Body Control

USE WITH:
Small groups

MATERIALS AND SUPPLIES

Several scooter boards
Several long scarves or pieces of fabric

Put the scarves in a container. Set them near the scooter boards.

ACTIVITY

Play **Scooter Board Tug** in partners. Each child sits on a scooter board facing the other one and holding onto opposite ends of a scarf. The children pull toward each other by pulling hand over hand on the scarf until they meet, and then they give each other a *"High-5!"*

VARIATIONS:

Lie Down and Pull: Have the children play **Scooter Board Tug** while lying on their stomachs or sitting on their knees on the scooter boards.

Say "Hello" Path

CHILDREN WILL DEVELOP
   Visual Motor Control
   Motor Planning
   Position in Space

USE WITH:
   Small groups
   Large groups

MATERIALS AND SUPPLIES

Long piece of rope or ball of thick rug yarn

ACTIVITY

Each child finds his own spot in the room. Be sure that everyone is spread out. Start the path by giving one end of the rope to a child to hold. Continue the path by going from child to child, having each one stay in his spot holding the rope. The path will zig-zag all around and across the room.

Ask one child to follow the path. The adult stands in the child's spot and holds onto his portion of the rope. The child starts at the beginning of the rope and follows the path with his hand, saying "*Hello,*" to each child he meets along the way. When he comes to the end of the path he chooses another child and stands in that child's spot and the game continues.

Sponge Ball Relays

MATERIALS AND SUPPLIES

Sponge balls

ACTIVITY

Divide the children into teams giving each team one sponge ball. Set up relays by having children hold their sponge balls in different positions such as:
- Between their knees, jumping, walking, sliding, etc.
- Under their chins, walking, running, sliding, skipping, or riding on trikes, hoppity hops, or scooter boards.
- Under their arms, walking, running, galloping, sliding, tiptoeing.
- Using two balls, one under each arm.

Clap for all of the children as they finish.

NOTE: If a child drops her ball, let her get it and continue the race. No starting over in **Sponge Ball Relays**!

VARIATIONS:

Sponge Ball Partners: Using partners, two children can hold a ball between them walking side by side, back to back, or head to head.

Push and Squish

CHILDREN WILL DEVELOP
  Body Coordination
  Visual Motor Coordination
  Body Awareness

USE WITH:
  Individuals
  Small groups

MATERIALS AND SUPPLIES
Different size sponge balls
Carpet squares
Velcro® tape

Put one side of your Velcro® tape on the sponge balls and the opposite side along your baseboards about 2-3 feet apart. Stick the balls on the baseboard.

ACTIVITY

Have the child sit on a carpet square facing the sponge ball with her hands placed behind her on the floor for support. Have her put her feet on the ball and push as hard as she can, trying to squish the ball against the wall. Have her relax and then push again and again and again.

NOTE: Encourage the children to:
● Push with both feet together on the ball at all times.
● Maintain their body positions and not rest on their elbows.

186

Pass the Ball

CHILDREN WILL DEVELOP
    Position in Space
    Motor Planning
    Visual Motor Control

USE WITH:
    Small groups
    Large groups

MATERIALS AND SUPPLIES

Objects to pass:
    Balls, various sizes and weights
    Bean bags
    Stuffed animals
    Cardboard blocks

ACTIVITY

This activity gives the children opportunities to bend, twist, turn, reach and make a variety of postural adjustments.

● Have them stand in a line approximately one foot apart and pass the object to each other:
  ● Over their heads,
  ● Through their legs, or
  ● Turning and passing the ball behind them.

● Have the children sit in a line on the floor or on chairs and pass the object to each other:
  ● Over their heads,
  ● Under their chairs, or
  ● Turning and passing the ball behind them.

● Have the children kneel on the floor keeping their bodies straight from the knees up. Have them pass the object to each other:
  ● Over their heads,
  ● Through their legs, or
  ● Turning and passing the ball behind them.

NOTE: Do this activity while the children are waiting for lunch, recess, bathroom, or other short waiting times.
Try it also for transition times. After each child passes the ball he leaves the group for the next activity.

Fun With Boxes

CHILDREN WILL DEVELOP
Visual Motor Control
Eye-Hand Coordination
Position in Space

USE WITH:
Individuals
Small groups

MATERIALS AND SUPPLIES

Several boxes, each one large enough for a child to sit in
Markers
Crayons
Stickers
Bingo markers
Stamps and stamp pad
Colored tape

Set several (2-3) boxes in a quiet area
of the room. Put the supplies on a tray.

ACTIVITY

Let a child sit or lie inside a box. Let her choose one or two markers, crayons, etc. and then decorate the inside of the box. Leave the boxes out for several days until they are completely decorated. Let the children use the boxes for individual activities, such as reading, writing, puzzles, thinking, etc.

NOTE: This activity is especially appropriate:
● For a child who needs to be separated from a large group.

● For a child who needs her own space.

Box Car

MATERIALS AND SUPPLIES

Several boxes large enough for a child to sit in
Masking tape
Stuffed animals
Large dolls

Using the masking tape, make a *"railroad track"* on the floor for the *"box cars"* to ride on. The track could run through your whole room, including loops, curves, circles, zig zags, and straight lines. Have a main depot where the *"engineers"* can park their *"box cars"* and hang their hats and coats.

ACTIVITY

Have the children find a partner to play **Box Car**. One child is the *passenger* and sits inside the box car. The other child is the *engineer* who pushes ("drives") the box car along the track. After the children have played for awhile, encourage them to park the box car in the depot and change places so that the *engineer* can have a ride. When everyone is finished park the box car in the depot for others to use.

VARIATIONS:

Stuffed Animal Ride: Have several chairs or a small bench in the depot. Place the stuffed animals and dolls on them. Let the *"engineers"* take these passengers for rides along the track.

Adventure Walk

CHILDREN WILL DEVELOP
Body Awareness
Motor Planning
Position in Space

USE WITH:
Small groups
Large groups

MATERIALS AND SUPPLIES

None

ACTIVITY

Have the children sit on the floor with their knees bent and their hands placed behind them on the floor for support. Tell the children an adventure story about a person or an animal. As you tell the story, let the children imitate the actions of the characters using their legs and feet, either on the floor or in the air. Include movements such as:
- Walking
- Running
- Kicking (an object such as a ball)
- Climbing up and down
- Sliding
- Skating
- Swinging

ALVIN GOES TO THE PARK

One day Alvin and his mother decided to go to the park. They walked slowly down the street, stopped at the corner, looked both ways for cars, and then walked quickly across the street. When they got to the park, Alvin ran to the swings and started to swing. The more he pumped, the higher he went. When he was tired of swinging he stopped, jumped off, and ran to the slide. He climbed up, up, up, up, up to the top and slid down. As they walked home, Alvin jumped over each crack in the sidewalk. (Continue.)

NOTE: When you read the words that are underlined, pause long enough for the children to imitate the actions of the legs and feet.

Shark

CHILDREN WILL DEVELOP
    Body Coordination
    Motor Planning
    Position in Space

USE WITH:
    Small groups
    Large groups

MATERIALS AND SUPPLIES

Large blanket, sheet, or parachute

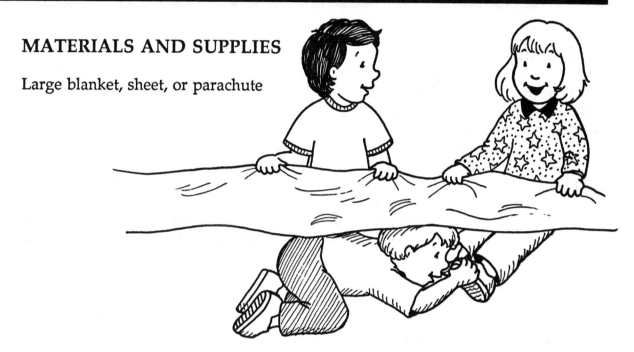

ACTIVITY

Ask the children to help you spread the blanket out on the floor. Have them sit around it with their legs underneath and their hands holding the edge. Hold the blanket slightly off the floor. Choose one child to be the "*Shark*."

The "*Shark*" crawls under the blanket, grabs one child's feet and pulls him "under" the blanket. (See NOTE.) Continue playing until all of the children are "under" the blanket.

NOTE: If a child does not want to go under the blanket, he can lie down and scoot under the blanket, so that his hands are under but his head stays outside.

VARIATIONS:

Shark Pool: Have several children pretend to be *sharks* at the same time. (This is especially appropriate for a large group of children.)

191

A Bumpy Roll

CHILDREN WILL DEVELOP
Body Coordination
Motor Planning
Position in Space

USE WITH:
Individuals
Small groups
Large groups

MATERIALS AND SUPPLIES

Large blanket or sheet
Variety of cushions, pillows, or pieces of foam
Large tumbling mat (optional)

ACTIVITY   Let the children help you randomly place a variety of
cushions, pillows, etc. on the floor/mat and cover them
with a large blanket. Have the children take turns rolling
across the blanket from one end to the other. Clap for each
child when he gets to the end of the mat.

VARIATIONS:
Move Along: Have the children walk, crawl, giant step,
tiptoe, somersault, or bounce across the blanket.

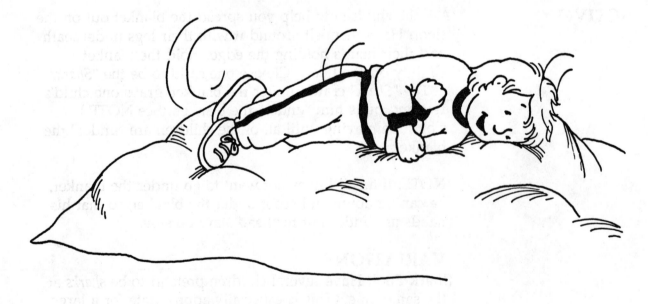

Obstacle Courses

CHILDREN WILL DEVELOP
Visual Motor Control
Motor Planning
Position in Space

USE WITH:
Individuals
Small groups
Large groups

MATERIALS AND SUPPLIES

Tumbling mats	Scooter boards	Blankets
Balance beams	Riding toys	Child-sized chairs
Mini-trampolines	Safety stilts	Ropes
Foam wedges	Blocks	Plastic grocery bags
Tunnels	Sofa cushions	Carpet squares
Barrels with open ends	Boxes	Large foam pieces

Each time you set up an obstacle course choose the materials and equipment you need. When planning and setting up the course remember:

● The purpose of an obstacle course is to provide the children with an environment to develop:
Motor planning
Postural adjustment
Balance
Coordination
Muscle tone

● When assessing and gathering equipment for the course, think of how you can use the materials to implement your targeted skills or gross motor movements. Incorporate a variety of equipment in the course to allow the children to practice gross motor movements such as:
Rolling
Crawling
Jumping
Spinning
Pulling
Mat movements

193

WAYS TO MOVE THROUGH AN OBSTACLE COURSE

ROLLING
- On a mat
- Over cushions
- Over inner tubes
- Inside a barrel
- Down a wedge or ramp

SPINNING
- On a sit and spin
- On a scooter board, sitting or lying
- On children's bottoms with their legs pulled up to their chests

WALKING
- Across a balance beam
- On a taped line
- On stilts
- On foam pieces

CRAWLING
- Over inner tubes
- Under a blanket
- Under a row of chairs
- Through a tunnel
- Through an open-ended barrel
- Through large appliance boxes
- Under a rope tied between chairs
- Through 4 or 5 inner tubes tied or taped together

JUMPING
- On a trampoline
- On a cushion
- On a taped line
- In a plastic grocery bag
- On an inner tube or row of tubes
- On a hoppity hop
- Over blocks, boxes, string, and balance beams

MORE WAYS TO MOVE THROUGH AN OBSTACLE COURSE

RIDING TOYS
- Big wheels
- Row carts
- Hoppity hops
- Child propelled cars
- Tricycles
- Scooter boards
- Scooter
- Flying turtles

NOTE: Have children ride these toys around safety cones, chairs, and other obstacles or follow a taped line on the floor.

PULLING
- Secure a rope at one or both ends and have the children pull themselves along the rope while sitting or lying on scooter boards.

STEPPING
- Inside holes of 4 to 6 inner tubes placed side by side
- Inside boxes of various sizes and heights placed side by side
- On a path of carpet squares
- Outlines of feet
- Small pieces of tape, staggered

MAT MOVEMENTS
- Log rolls
- Egg roll
- Seal walk
- Duck walk
- Crab walk
- Wheelbarrow
- Forward somersault

SAMPLE OBSTACLE COURSE FOR A LARGE AREA
SUCH AS A GYM OR OUTSIDE

- Crawl through a tunnel
- Ride a hoppity hop along a taped line
- Jump on a mini-trampoline
- Roll across a mat
- Walk across a balance beam
- Pull self while lying on a scooter board
- Walk on a taped line wearing stilts

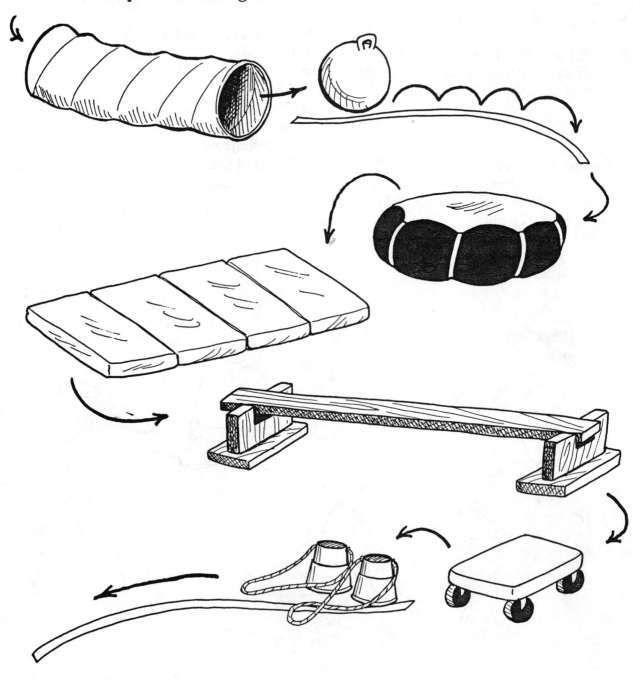

SAMPLE OBSTACLE COURSE FOR A SMALL AREA
SUCH AS YOUR CLASSROOM

- Walk around a safety cone
- Duck walk along a taped line
- Hop over several cardboard blocks one at a time
- Climb in and out of a box
- Crawl over a tube
- Jump up and down in a plastic grocery bag

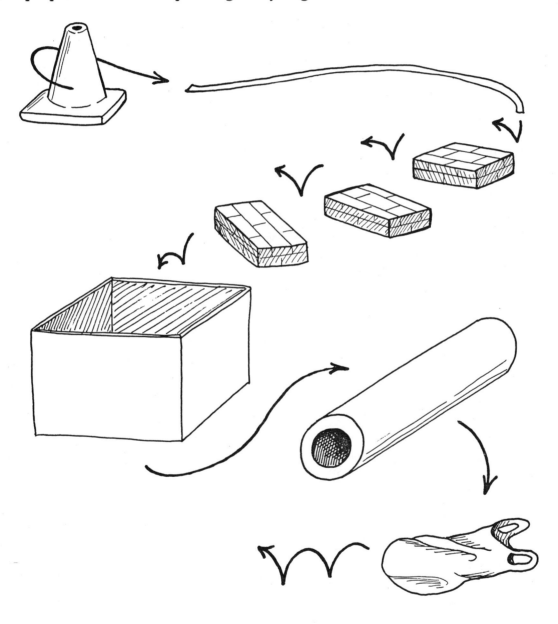

APPENDIXES

- GLOSSARY OF TERMS

- SUPPLIES

- RECIPES

GLOSSARY of TERMS

- Fine Motor

- Oral Motor

- Visual Control

- Gross Motor

The ideas in **ACTIVITIES UNLIMITED** are based on the knowledge of how children's sensory and motor systems work together to affect behavior. Children's behavior and thinking capabilities are reflections of the function of their central nervous system. A well integrated nervous system allows children to receive sensory information from their environment and from their own bodies and to use that information to produce a motor or social response. Automatic or non-thinking portions of the brain which receive sensations (touch, information tendons, muscles and joints, pain, and movement) and intellectual thinking portions (needed for academics and perceptual processing) must work in concert.

It is the ability of the nervous system to recognize information from within the body and from the environment, organize, and delete the unnecessary so that only the most essential information is retained to guide an individual to respond appropriately to a task.

ARM, HAND, FINGER COORDINATION

is the ability to coordinate movements of the arm, hand, and fingers in ways that promote fine motor skills.

> ARM, HAND, FINGER COORDINATION is necessary to promote daily living skills such as fastening buttons and taking off the top of a tube of toothpaste. It is necessary for many play skills such as putting pegs in a pegboard, putting puzzles together, and building with blocks.

BODY AWARENESS

is knowledge of individual body parts, their position and movement in space, and how body parts are used in different combinations to perform tasks.

> BODY AWARENESS is necessary to participate in self-help (getting dressed), work (washing a table), and play (playing on the playground) activities.

BODY COORDINATION

is the ability to move all parts of the body together in a smooth fluid manner. This includes the upper and lower portions of the body, the two sides of the body, or any single body part.

> BODY COORDINATION is necessary to run, kick, catch, and swing.

BREATH CONTROL

is regulating air an individual uses to eat, to speak clearly and loudly in conversation, and to direct and sustain the pushing out and drawing in of air for blowing and sucking activities.

> **BREATH CONTROL** is necessary to sing, speak in sentences, drink through a straw, and blow out birthday candles.

CONTROL OF FACIAL MUSCLES, JAWS, AND LIPS

is the capacity to control the amount and direction of movement of these facial parts.

> **CONTROL OF FACIAL MUSCLES, JAWS, AND LIPS** is necessary to produce intelligible speech and to refine sucking, biting, chewing, and lip control.

EYE-HAND COORDINATION

is the connection between the eyes and the hands that allows the eyes to sight and focus before and during any movement of the hand. The eyes determine the plan of movement and give the necessary feedback before and during each movement of the hand.

> **EYE-HAND COORDINATION** is necessary to do motor tasks such as cutting, eatintg with utensils, stringing beads, popping bubbles, sewing, and catching balls.

FACIAL AWARENESS

is the general knowledge of the position and movement of the cheeks, tongue, lips, teeth, and jaw.

> **FACIAL AWARENESS** is necessary to notice that ice cream is running down your chin, that you've been kissed, and that your nose is running or you are drooling.

FINGER COORDINATION

is the ability to move the fingers of the hand together in many combinations to grasp or manipulate an object of any shape, size, or weight to perform a specific task.

> **FINGER COORDINATION** is necessary to color, use utensils, manipulate play dough, and write.

HAND COORDINATION

involves the ability to shape the hand around or move objects using a combination of the palm of the hand with one or more fingers and thumb. This ability may include moving an object within the hand or in the environment.

> **HAND COORDINATION** is necessary to manipulate objects such as puzzle pieces, legos, clay, and toy cars. It promotes the ability to care for oneself, such as zipping your coat, tieing your shoes, opening lids or tops to containers.

HAND CONTROL

is the ability to choose the best way to hold, position, and move objects (of different shapes, sizes, and textures), how tight your grasp should be, and when to change grasp patterns from the whole hand to just fingers and thumb.

> **HAND CONTROL** is necessary to use tools such as a hair brush, a pencil, or a pair of scissors. It is also necessary for daily living skills such as using a knife, fork, and spoon.

HAND STRENGTH

is the ability to use sufficient and grade muscle strength in the forearm and hand to hold, move, and use objects of varying sizes and weights.

> **HAND STRENGTH** is necessary to use tools in daily life such as a stapler, hole punch, and scissors or to open a milk carton or a box of cereal.

MOTOR PLANNING

is the ability to have an idea, plan and move the body in a new way to perform unfamiliar activities and tasks, or to use tools for the first time.

> **MOTOR PLANNING** is necessary to climb on the monkey bars, play hopscotch, move through an obstacle course, and play group games.

POSITION IN SPACE

is the knowledge of where your body is and knowing how to change that position during an activity.

> **POSITION IN SPACE** is necessary to hit or catch a ball, walk down the hall or through the classroom, play games in the gym or on the playground, jump rope, or ride a bike

TACTILE AWARENESS

is the ability to use the receptors in the skin to acknowledge the body, and to identify when an object or person has touched a particular part of the body.

> **TACTILE AWARENESS** is necessary to know whether your clothes are wet, you have food on your face, someone has bumped into you or tapped you on the shoulder.

TACTILE DISCRIMINATION

is the ability to use the receptors in the skin to interpret information about one's own body and the qualities and characteristics of objects that touch the skin. Basic tactile discrimination protects the body from harm and more mature tactile discrimination gives you more details about what was touched.

> **TACTILE DISCRIMINATION** is necessary to develop the ability to recognize by touch the difference between hot and cold, soft and hard, sharp and dull, a pencil, crayon, or marker, a scissors or paper punch, and to determine if shoes are on the correct feet or clothes are on backwards.

TONGUE CONTROL

is the ability to intentionally move the entire tongue in or out, from side to side, up and down, and have it rest inside the mouth.

> **TONGUE CONTROL** is necessary to pronounce words correctly, eat, drink from a straw, lick a popsicle or lollipop, chew gum, and move food inside the mouth to be chewed.

UPPER BODY CONTROL

is control of the upper part of the body including the head, neck, shoulders, arms, and trunk.

> **UPPER BODY CONTROL** is necessary for eye-hand coordination, arm, hand and finger coordination, and visual control. It enables a person to sit on a chair or at a table and to coordinate the movements of arms away from the body in order to write, draw, color, read, build things, etc.

VISUAL CONTROL

is the ability to control the muscles of the eyes together to focus on, and follow or find objects in the environment. This includes seeing something close, far away, and maintaining visual contact.

> **VISUAL CONTROL** is necessary to imitate fingerplays and copy from the blackboard, or follow the action in a group game.

VISUAL MEMORY

is the ability to create a mental image of something that has been seen previously.

> **VISUAL MEMORY** is necessary for a person to remember, to talk about or draw a picture of a past experience, to play Concentration, to read, to spell, etc.

VISUAL MOTOR CONTROL

is the capacity to use the eyes and hands together for specific tasks. The eyes always sight first directing the movement of the entire body, arm, hand, or small body part.

> **VISUAL MOTOR CONTROL** is necessary to write on a line, trace, draw, color inside lines, and bounce a ball.

VISUAL MOTOR COORDINATION

is the ability of the eyes and any part of the body to work together to produce smooth, controlled, precise movements needed for skilled activity.

> **VISUAL MOTOR COORDINATION** is necessary to kick a ball, cook, build objects, play tag, and ride a bike on a sidewalk.

SUPPLIES

- •Equipment
- •Materials
- •Consumables

EQUIPMENT

Balance beams

Balls, various sizes and weights

Barrels with open ends

Blocks, cardboard and wooden

Carpet squares

Chairs

Dish tubs

Doll clothes

Dolls

Drums

Full-length mirror

Hoppity hops

Inner tubes

Mini-trampolines

Record player

Riding toys

Rugs

Safety stilts

Scooter boards

Small plastic swimming pool

Smocks

Stools

Stuffed animals

Trucks

Tumbling mats

Tunnels

Vehicles

Wash tubs

Waste baskets

Water table

Building Blocks 38W567 Brindlewood ~ Elgin, IL 60123

MATERIALS

Baseball gloves	Cushions
Beachballs	Erasers
Bean bags	Eye droppers
Bed sheet	Feather dusters
Bingo chips	Flashlight
Bingo markers	Funnels
Blankets	Giant paper clips
Bowling pins	Gloves
Boxing gloves	Heavy cardboard tubes
Brownie pans	Hole punches
Bubble wands	Ice cube trays
Bubble pack	Jewelry
Buckets	Magnetic bingo chips
Buttons	Magnetic bingo wands
Clothesline	Marbles
Clothespins	Measuring cups
Colored inch cubes	Mittens
Cookie sheets	Muffin pans
Corks	Oven mittens
Crates	Paint brushes

Paint rollers

Pie pans

Pillow cases

Pillows

Ping-pong balls

Pitcher

Plastic spray bottles

Plastic boats

Plastic squeeze containers

Poker chips

Puppets

Purses

Rhythm sticks

Rubber hand exercisers

Rubber stamps and pads

Rubber gloves

Scarves

Scissors

Scoops

Shells

Shoes

Shovels

Snack bag clips

Sofa cushions

Sponge balls

Sponges

Spoons

Stamp pads

Stencils

Straight pins

Strainers

Teddy bear counters

Tongs

Towels

Trays

Turkey basters

Tweezers

Washcloths

Wedge cushions

Yarn balls

Building Blocks 38W567 Brindlewood ~ Elgin, IL 60123

CONSUMABLE

Adding machine tape

Aluminum foil

Aquarium gravel

Bird seed

Blue liquid starch

Boxes

Bubble mixture

Cardboard, all types

Cardboard milk cartons

Cardboard tubes

Cereal boxes

Chalk

Clear plastic tubing

Clear plastic wrap

Coffee cans

Coffee can lids

Coffee grounds

Colored tape

Construction paper, all colors

Cornstarch

Cotton balls

Crayons

Disposable cups

Duct tape

Egg cartons

Extra-firm balloons,
   inflatable punch balls

Extracts

Fabrics

Film containers

Fingerpaint

Food coloring

Hand lotion

Hangers

Index cards

Ivory Snow® powder

Liquid dish detergent

Liquid hand soap

Long plastic *"sleeves"* in which
   newspapers are delivered

Margarine containers

Markers, all colors

Masking tape

SUPPLIES

Meat trays

Napkins

Paper plates

Paper grocery bags

Paper lunch bags

Paper, all types

Party favor blowouts

Patterned adhesive paper

Pencils

Perfume

Petroleum jelly

Playdough

Popsicle sticks

Posterboard, all colors

Powder without talc

Rubber bands

Salt

Sand

Sandpaper

Sandwich bags

Sawdust

Scents

Scouring pads

Self-adhesive Velcro® dots

Shaving cream

Sheets of packing foam

Shoe boxes

Slide frames

Soap crayons

Stamps

Stickers

Sticky dots and stamps

Straws

String

Telephone wire

Tongue depressors

Toothpicks

Twine

Velcro® tape

Wallpaper

White glue

Yarn

Building Blocks 38W567 Brindlewood ~ Elgin, IL 60123

RECIPES

- Playdough
- Soap Crayons
- Silly Putty
- Washable Make-Up
- Bubble Brew

PLAYDOUGH

Supplies

5 Cups Flour
1 Cup Salt
4T Alum
2T Vegetable Oil
3 Cups Water
Food Coloring (optional)

Make

1. Boil the water. (Add food coloring to the water if you want colored dough.)

2. Mix vegetable oil and all dry ingredients in a large bowl.

3. Add the boiling water.

4. Stir ingredients together.

5. When cool enough put the dough on the table and knead until it is thoroughly mixed.

6. Store the Playdough in a tightly covered container.

BUILDING BLOCKS 38W567 Brindlewood ~ Elgin, IL 60123

SOAP CRAYONS

Supplies

1 Cup Soap Flakes
1/8 Cup Water
Food Coloring

Make

1. Pour the water into a cup and add the food coloring.

2. Pour the liquid into a mixing bowl.

3. Add the soap flakes.

4. Mix well.

5. Press the mixture into sections of an ice cube tray.

6. Let the mixture sit for several days and then pop out the crayons.

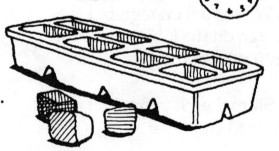

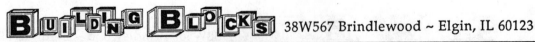
BUILDING BLOCKS 38W567 Brindlewood ~ Elgin, IL 60123

SILLY PUTTY

Supplies

1 Cup White Glue
1 Cup Liquid Starch
(Sta-Flo)

Make

1. Pour the glue and starch into a large bowl.

2. Mix them together using a heavy-duty spoon.

3. If the mixture is too thin add more glue.

4. If the mixture is too thick add more starch.

5. Store the Silly Putty in a tightly covered container or plastic bag.

38W567 Brindlewood ~ Elgin, IL 60123

WASHABLE MAKE-UP

Supplies

4T White Shortening
10T Cornstarch
2T Flour
Food Coloring

Make

1. Mix the shortening, cornstarch, and flour with a mixer until it is a paste-like consistency.

2. Divide the paste into smaller portions.

3. Mix each portion with a few drops of food coloring for a variety of colors.

4. Use your fingers to apply the make-up. Remove it with cold cream, shortening, or baby oil.

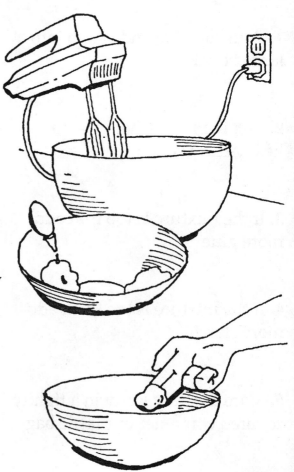

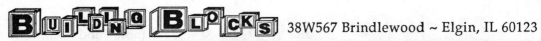

38W567 Brindlewood ~ Elgin, IL 60123

BUBBLE BREW

Supplies

1 Quart Water
3/4 Cup Liquid Detergent
   (Dawn or Joy)
1/4 Cup Corn Syrup

Make

1. Mix the water, detergent, and corn syrup in a large bowl.

2. Let the mixture sit overnight. (at least 6 hours)

3. Store the Bubble Brew in a covered bowl. Keep in the refrigerator.

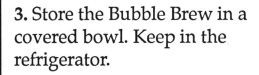 38W567 Brindlewood ~ Elgin, IL 60123

FOR EVERY MONTH

BUILDING BLOCKS

an activity newspaper for adults
and their young children

**TAKE
A LOOK
AT
BUILDING
BLOCKS
NEWSPAPER**

PUBLISHED:
10 times a year
including an expanded
summer issue.

RATES:
1 Year ~ $20⁰⁰
2 Years ~ $36⁵⁰
3 Years ~ $50⁰⁰
Sample ~ $ 3⁰⁰

SEND YOUR NAME, ADDRESS
(INCLUDING ZIP CODE), AND
PAYMENT TO:

BUILDING BLOCKS
38W567 Brindlewood
Elgin, Il   60123

BUILDING BLOCKS is a 20 page early
childhood activity newspaper offering a total
curriculum resource to use in your classroom
and share with your parents.

MONTHLY FEATURES include:

~ Reproducible parent activity calendar.

~ Activity pages highlighting language, art,
physical, science/math, creative, and self/social
activities which are easy to plan and
implement.

~ Ready-to-use charts, games, and/or posters.

~ Special activity page for toddlers and twos.

~ Large easy-to-use illustrations.

~ 4 page **FEATURED TOPIC** *Pull-Out Section.*

Building Blocks Library

The Circle Time Series

by Liz and Dick Wilmes. Hundreds of activities for large and small groups of children. Each book is filled with Language and Active games, Fingerplays, Songs, Stories, Snacks, and more. A great resource for every library shelf.

Circle Time Book
Captures the spirit of 39 holidays and seasons.
ISBN 0-943452-00-7   **$ 9.95**

Everyday Circle Times
Over 900 ideas. Choose from 48 topics divided into 7 sections: self-concept, basic concepts, animals, foods, science, occupations, and recreation.
ISBN 0-943452-01-5   **$14.95**

More Everyday Circle Times
Divided into the same 7 sections as EVERYDAY. Features new topics such as Birds and Pizza, plus all new ideas for some familiar topics contained in EVERYDAY.
ISBN 0-943452-14-7   **$14.95**

Yearful of Circle Times
52 different topics to use weekly, by seasons, or mixed throughout the year. New Friends, Signs of Fall, Snowfolk Fun, and much more.
ISBN 0-943452-10-4   **$14.95**

Paint Without Brushes

by Liz and Dick Wilmes. Use common materials which you already have to discover the painting possibilities in your classroom! PAINT WITHOUT BRUSHES gives your children open-ended art activities to explore paint in lots of creative ways. A valuable art resource. One you'll want to use daily.
ISBN 0-943452-15-5   **$12.95**

Gifts, Cards, and Wraps

by Wilmes and Zavodsky. Help the children sparkle with the excitement of gift giving. Filled with thoughtful gifts, unique wraps, and special cards which the children can make and give. They're sure to bring smiles.
ISBN 0-943452-06-6   **$ 7.95**

Everyday Bulletin Boards

by Wilmes and Moehling. Features borders, murals, backgrounds, and other open-ended art to display on your bulletin boards. Plus board ideas with patterns, which teachers can make and use to enhance their curriculum.
ISBN 0-943452-09-0   **$ 8.95**

Exploring Art

by Liz and Dick Wilmes. EXPLORING ART is divided by months. Over 250 art ideas for paint, chalk, doughs, scissors, and more. Easy to set-up in your classroom.
ISBN 0-943452-05-8   **$16.95**

CIRCLE TIME

ART

Parachute Play

by Liz and Dick Wilmes. A year 'round approach to one of the most versatile pieces of large muscle equipment. Starting with basic techniques, PARACHUTE PLAY provides over 100 activities to use with your parachute.
ISBN 0-943452-03-1 $ 7.95

Classroom Parties

by Susan Spaete. Each party plan suggests decorations, trimmings, and snacks which the children can easily make to set a festive mood. Choose from games, songs, art activities, stories, and related experiences which will add to the spirit and fun.
ISBN 0-943452-07-4 $ 8.95

Imagination Stretchers

by Liz and Dick Wilmes. Perfect for whole language. Over 400 conversation starters for creative discussions, simple lists, and beginning dictation and writing.
ISBN 0-943452-04-X $ 6.95

Parent Programs and Open Houses

by Susan Spaete. Filled with a wide variety of year 'round presentations, pre-registration ideas, open houses, and end-of-the-year gatherings. All involve the children from the planning stages through the programs.
ISBN 0-943452-08-2 $ 9.95

Learning Centers

by Liz and Dick Wilmes. Hundreds of open-ended activities to quickly involve and excite your children. You'll use it every time you plan and whenever you need a quick, additional activity. A must for every teacher's bookshelf.
ISBN 0-943452-13-9 $16.95

Felt Board Fun

by Liz and Dick Wilmes. Make your felt board come alive. Discover how versatile it is as the children become involved with a wide range of activities. This unique book has over 150 ideas with accompanying patterns.
ISBN 0-943452-02-3 $14.95

Table & Floor Games

by Liz and Dick Wilmes. 32 easy-to-make, fun-to-play table/floor games with accompanying patterns ready to trace or photocopy. Teach beginning concepts such as matching, counting, colors, alphabet recognition, sorting and so on.
ISBN 0-943452-16-3 $16.95

Activities Unlimited

by Adler, Caton, and Cleveland. Create an enthusiasm for learning! Hundreds of innovative activities to help your children develop fine and gross motor skills, increase their language, become self-reliant, and play cooperatively. Whether you're a beginning teacher or a veteran, this book will quickly become one of your favorites.
ISBN 0-943452-17-1 $16.95

2'S Experience Series

by Liz and Dick Wilmes. An exciting series developed especially for toddlers and twos!

2's Experience - Felt Board Fun

Make your felt board come alive. Enjoy stories, activities, and rhymes developed just for very young children. Hundreds of extra large patterns feature teddy bears, birthdays, farm animals, and much, much more.
ISBN0-943452-19-8   **$12.95**

2's Experience - Fingerplays

A wonderful collection of easy fingerplays with accompanying games and large FINGERPLAY CARDS. Put each CARD together so that your children can look at the picture on one side, while you look at the words and actions on the other. Build a CARD file to use everyday.
ISBN 0-943452-18-X   **$9.95**

Watch for more titles in the 2's Experience series.

All books available from teacher stores, school supply catalogs or directly from:

Thank you for your order.

38W567 Brindlewood
Elgin, Illinois 60123
800-233-2448   708-742-1054 (FAX)

	Each	Total
BUILDING BLOCKS Subscription	20.00	_____
2's EXPERIENCE Series		
2'S EXPERIENCE FELTBOARD FUN	12.95	_____
2'S EXPERIENCE FINGERPLAYS	9.95	_____
CIRCLE TIME Series		
CIRCLE TIME BOOK	9.95	_____
EVERYDAY CIRCLE TIMES	14.95	_____
MORE EVERYDAY CIRCLE TIMES	14.95	_____
YEARFUL OF CIRCLE TIMES	14.95	_____
ART		
PAINT WITHOUT BRUSHES	12.95	_____
EXPLORING ART	16.95	_____
EVERYDAY BULLETIN BOARDS	8.95	_____
GIFTS, CARDS, AND WRAPS	7.95	_____
LEARNING GAMES		
ACTIVITIES UNLIMITED	14.95	_____
FELT BOARD FUN	14.95	_____
TABLE & FLOOR GAMES	16.95	_____
LEARNING CENTERS	16.95	_____
ASSORTED TITLES		
CLASSROOM PARTIES	8.95	_____
IMAGINATION STRETCHERS	6.95	_____
PARACHUTE PLAY	7.95	_____
PARENT PROGRAMS/OPEN HOUSE	9.95	_____
	TOTAL	_____

Name_____

Address _____

City_____

State_____ Zip _____

QUALITY BUILDING BLOCKS SINCE 1977